Modern Web Testing with TestCafe

Get to grips with end-to-end web testing with
TestCafe and JavaScript

Dmytro Shpakovskyi

BIRMINGHAM—MUMBAI

Modern Web Testing with TestCafe

Commissioning Editor: Pavan Ramchandani
Acquisition Editor: Nitin Nainani
Senior Editor: Hayden Edwards
Content Development Editor: Aamir Ahmed
Technical Editor: Shubham Sharma
Copy Editor: Safis Editing
Project Coordinator: Kinjal Bari
Proofreader: Safis Editing
Indexer: Manju Arasan
Production Designer: Joshua Misquitta

First published: September 2020

Production reference: 2050521

Published by Packt Publishing Ltd.
Livery Place
35 Livery Street
Birmingham
B3 2PB, UK.

ISBN 978-1-80020-095-1

www.packt.com

I have to start by thanking my awesome wife, Julie. Thank you for your patience. Thanks to everyone on the Packt team who helped me so much. Special thanks to Divij, the always-on-track Project Manager, and Hayden, the greatest editor I could ever imagine.

– Dmytro Shpakovskyi

Contributors

About the author

Dmytro Shpakovskyi has over 10 years of experience in the **quality assurance (QA)**, software testing, and software-as-a-service industries. Skilled in end-to-end, load, and API test automation, he is certified by the ISTQB.

During his successful career, Dmytro has led on QA automation for a platform of 60+ highly scalable web applications and services, built and maintained numerous test automation frameworks, managed distributed teams of QA automation engineers, mentored, and helped to convert manual test engineers to test automation.

You can often find Dmytro creating and open-sourcing new test automation frameworks, mentoring other QA engineers, or exploring new tools and techniques for automated testing. He shares his experience at `stijit.com`.

About the reviewer

Dzimitry Mikhnevich is highly experienced in manual testing, test automation, load and performance testing, and API testing. He holds the position of QA Automation in one of the largest IT companies in Russia. During his career, he has mastered a number of testing tools, including TestCafe. Dzimitry participates in the development of several projects aimed at improving the testing of internal products of the company he's part of.

Packt is searching for authors like you

If you're interested in becoming an author for Packt, please visit `authors.packtpub.com` and apply today. We have worked with thousands of developers and tech professionals, just like you, to help them share their insight with the global tech community. You can make a general application, apply for a specific hot topic that we are recruiting an author for, or submit your own idea.

Table of Contents

4

Building a Test Suite with TestCafe

5

Improving the Tests

Preface

TestCafe is a self-sufficient, free, and open source end-to-end testing framework that combines unmatched ease of use with advanced automation and robust built-in stability mechanisms. It can be used to write fast and reliable tests.

Modern Web Testing with TestCafe is a comprehensive, project-based introduction for those who are new to TestCafe. You'll build a suite of end-to-end tests while learning the core methods and concepts along the way.

You'll learn how to write end-to-end tests using the TestCafe syntax, and the features of the TestCafe framework. You'll go from setting up the environment all the way to writing production-ready tests. Throughout the book, we'll build a sample set of tests step by step that will log in to the website, verify the elements present on different pages, create/delete entities, and execute custom JavaScript code, using TestCafe. Additionally, there will be several stages of refactoring, to showcase setup/teardown and PageObjects. While this test suite is relatively simple to build, it allows some of the most prominent features of TestCafe to be showcased. Additionally, it demonstrates the running of the tests against a free and simple-to-use website, and it does not require readers to build and deploy their own servers or backend services.

By the end of this book, you will know how to write and enhance end-to-end tests with TestCafe in order to solve real-world problems and deliver results. You'll also have a proof of concept to demonstrate to others.

Disclaimer:

Please note the book is not written or produced by Developer Express Inc. Developer Express Inc is not affiliated with Packt and the book is copyright of Packt Publishing Pvt. Ltd.

Who this book is for

This book is intended for quality assurance engineers, test automation engineers, software engineers in test, SDETs, and software project managers interested in using TestCafe for test automation. Full stack software developers and professionals responsible for creating enterprise-based testing frameworks will also find this useful. A basic knowledge of JavaScript/Node.js, CSS selectors, HTML and Bash is necessary.

What this book covers

Chapter 1, *Why TestCafe?*, explains what TestCafe is and what its main features are.

Chapter 2, *Exploring TestCafe under the Hood*, takes a deeper dive into how TestCafe works and what secrets are hidden under its hood.

Chapter 3, *Setting Up the Environment*, covers how to set up the environment in order to run the tests.

Chapter 4, *Building a Test Suite with TestCafe*, explains, having covered the main concepts of TestCafe and reviewed its arsenal, how to draw a weapon and write some tests.

Chapter 5, *Improving the Tests*, covers how to extend the tests and add setup and teardown.

Chapter 6, *Refactoring with PageObjects*, covers how to make the tests more effective and transparent by refactoring with PageObjects.

Chapter 7, *Findings from TestCafe*, provides a quick overview of what lies ahead.

To get the most out of this book

The following table shows the minimum software requirements for this book:

Software covered in the book	OS requirements
TestCafe	Windows, macOS, Linux (any)
ECMAScript 6+ (also known as ES6+ and ECMAScript 2015+)	Windows, macOS, Linux (any)

If you are using the digital version of this book, we advise you to type the code yourself or access the code via the GitHub repository (link available in the next section). Doing so will help you avoid any potential errors related to the copying and pasting of code.

Download the example code files

You can download the example code files for this book from your account at www. packt.com. If you purchased this book elsewhere, you can visit www.packtpub.com/ support and register to have the files emailed directly to you.

You can download the code files by following these steps:

1. Log in or register at www.packt.com.

2. Select the **Support** tab.

3. Click on **Code Downloads**.

4. Enter the name of the book in the **Search** box and follow the onscreen instructions.

Once the file is downloaded, please make sure that you unzip or extract the folder using the latest version of:

- WinRAR/7-Zip for Windows.

- Zipeg/iZip/UnRarX for Mac.

- 7-Zip/PeaZip for Linux.

The code bundle for the book is also hosted on GitHub at https://github.com/ PacktPublishing/Modern-Web-Testing-with-TestCafe. In case there's an update to the code, it will be updated on the existing GitHub repository.

We also have other code bundles from our rich catalog of books and videos available at https://github.com/PacktPublishing/. Check them out!

Conventions used

There are a number of text conventions used throughout this book.

Code in text: Indicates code words in text, database table names, folder names, filenames, file extensions, pathnames, dummy URLs, user input, and Twitter handles. Here is an example: 'Open basic-tests.js in a code editor (or IDE) of your choice and let's create a simple test.'

A block of code is set as follows:

```
const { Selector } = require('testcafe');

fixture('My first set of tests');

test('My first test', async (t) => {
    // Your test code
});
```

Any command-line input or output is written as follows:

```
$ cd test-project/
$ mkdir tests
```

Bold: Indicates a new term, an important word, or words that you see on screen. For example, words in menus or dialog boxes appear in the text like this. Here is an example: 'Expected result: **'Issue created'** notification should be displayed:'

> **Tips or important notes**
> Appear like this.

Get in touch

Feedback from our readers is always welcome.

General feedback: If you have questions about any aspect of this book, mention the book title in the subject of your message and email us at `customercare@packtpub.com`.

Errata: Although we have taken every care to ensure the accuracy of our content, mistakes do happen. If you have found a mistake in this book, we would be grateful if you would report this to us. Please visit `www.packtpub.com/support/errata`, selecting your book, clicking on the Errata Submission Form link, and entering the details.

Piracy: If you come across any illegal copies of our works in any form on the internet, we would be grateful if you would provide us with the location address or website name. Please contact us at `copyright@packt.com` with a link to the material.

If you are interested in becoming an author: If there is a topic that you have expertise in, and you are interested in either writing or contributing to a book, please visit `authors.packtpub.com`.

Reviews

Please leave a review. Once you have read and used this book, why not leave a review on the site that you purchased it from? Potential readers can then see and use your unbiased opinion to make purchase decisions, we at Packt can understand what you think about our products, and our authors can see your feedback on their book. Thank you!

For more information about Packt, please visit `packt.com`.

1
Why TestCafe?

TestCafe—a new promising software testing framework or just a place where you can eat? Here, we will take a look at what TestCafe is and what its main features are. What is the technology? What do you need to know? How does it integrate with other tools? In this book, we will see what TestCafe is used for, go through its main features, and compare it with a well-known industry standard—Selenium.

More practically, we will develop a set of tests for a bug tracking system. You will learn how to write end-to-end tests using the TestCafe syntax and the features of the TestCafe framework. You'll go from setting up the environment all the way down to writing production-ready tests.

Throughout this book, we'll build a sample set of tests step by step that will log in to a website, verify the elements present on different pages, create/delete entities, and execute custom JavaScript code using TestCafe. Additionally, there will be several stages of refactoring to showcase setup/teardown and PageObjects.

> **Note**
>
> Please keep in mind that this book does not pretend to be the only source of truth - its main goal is to demonstrate some original approaches, not to enforce the strict rules. Feel free to use and extend all the techniques explored in this book.

By the end of this chapter, we will have a clear idea of TestCafe and what lies ahead—a plan of features that will be tested. We will also review the demo website and come up with a set of test cases that will be automated in the upcoming chapters.

To sum up the contents of this chapter, the following main topics will be covered:

- Introducing TestCafe.
- Exploring the main features of TestCafe.
- Comparing TestCafe and Selenium.
- Reviewing the test project we will build.

Introducing TestCafe

If you work for a huge enterprise company or a small but innovative start-up and your automated tests need to support customers with older browsers the same as the new ones, you should definitely try TestCafe. Just like Selenium, it's open source, but you don't have to install any other packages or additional web drivers. TestCafe is a self-sufficient, free, end-to-end testing framework that combines unmatched ease of use with advanced automation and robust built-in stability mechanisms.

It was created by DevExpress (`https://github.com/DevExpress`) and was open sourced under the MIT license. TestCafe can take care of all stages of the automated testing process:

- Launching applications before tests.
- Launching different browsers.
- Running tests.
- Taking screenshots.
- Outputting test results.

TestCafe does not require any additional installation of browser plugins and works in all major modern browsers right out of the box. It is gaining popularity as a faster and easier-to-use solution compared to Selenium.

Now that we've had a quick glimpse of what TestCafe is, let's continue with an overview of its main features.

Exploring the main features of TestCafe

Now, let's take a more detailed look at all the bells and whistles that TestCafe has to offer:

- Pretty much all TestCafe needs to run is a browser and Node.js configured on your machine, so there is **minimal setup**.

- TestCafe can run tests in **headless mode** (on Chrome or Firefox) without a need to render a **Document Object Model (DOM)**. This feature is extremely useful when running tests on any **Continuous Integration (CI)** system.

- TestCafe **supports all main operating systems**, including Windows, macOS, and Linux.

- The officially supported browsers of TestCafe are Google Chrome (Stable, Beta, Dev, and Canary), Internet Explorer (11+), Microsoft Edge (Legacy and Chromium-based), Mozilla Firefox, Safari, Google Chrome mobile, and Safari mobile – so it is **cross-browser**. You can find a full list of supported browsers and their aliases at `https://devexpress.github.io/testcafe/documentation/guides/concepts/browsers.html#officially-supported-browsers`.

- Tests can be written in the latest **JavaScript (ES6+), TypeScript,** or **CoffeeScript** formats (we will be using JavaScript to demonstrate this in the upcoming chapters).

- Clear and flexible API with support of the **PageModel pattern** (we will see how this works in *Chapter 6, Refactoring with PageObjects*).

- Stable tests due to the **smart assertion and automatic waiting mechanisms** (this will be discussed in *Chapter 2, Exploring TestCafe Under the Hood*).

- TestCafe has a lot of **free custom plugins**: cloud browser providers and emulators (SauceLabs, BrowserStack, CrossBrowserTesting, and so on), framework-specific selectors to interact with page elements in a way that is native to your framework (React, Angular, Vue, and Aurelia), custom reporters to get test results in different formats (TeamCity, Slack, NUnit, and TimeCafe), IDE plugins to run tests and view results from your favorite IDE (Visual Studio Code, Webstorm, and SublimeText), Cucumber support to create and run tests with Cucumber syntax, and much more, as TestCafe developers and community members are extremely active. All of these are ready to use and open source (`https://github.com/DevExpress/testcafe#plugins`).

These are the main features of the TestCafe open source framework. Wondering if there are any products on top of that that don't require you to write code? Sure thing!

Introducing TestCafe Studio

In addition to the open source TestCafe framework, there is a paid test recording tool called TestCafe Studio. It is built on top of the TestCafe engine to give test engineers the opportunity to record, run, and update tests without any special knowledge of JavaScript. It is achieved by transforming user actions from recording into repeatable code.

As well as complementing the features provided by the TestCafe framework, TestCafe Studio takes things even further with the following:

- **Visual test recorder**: This allows you to create tests without writing any code. It records your interactions with the web page in the browser and generates corresponding tests (`https://docs.devexpress.com/TestCafeStudio/400165/guides/record-tests`).

- **Interactive test editor**: Allows you to view and edit tests and hooks in a comprehensive, visualized manner (`https://docs.devexpress.com/TestCafeStudio/400190/user-interface/test-editor`).

- **Automatic selector generation**: TestCafe Studio can generate element selectors while recording when you interact with a web page or when a web page element is picked with the element picker (`https://docs.devexpress.com/TestCafeStudio/400407/test-actions/element-selectors#auto-generated-element-selectors`).

- **Run configuration manager**: Allows you to create, modify, and delete run configurations for desktop, headless, and mobile browsers (`https://docs.devexpress.com/TestCafeStudio/400189/user-interface/run-configurations-dialog`).

- **Code editor**: Allows you to write and modify test scripts (`https://docs.devexpress.com/TestCafeStudio/400181/user-interface/code-editor`).

> **Note**
>
> TestCafe Studio has 30-day free trial period – you can find more information about this at `https://www.devexpress.com/products/testcafestudio/qa-end-to-end-web-testing.xml`.

Let's stop for a moment, catch our breath, and review what we have learned so far. We have acquired a basic understanding of what TestCafe is and have gone through a list of what it has to offer – the main features, plugins, and the TestCafe Studio test recording tool. Now, let's proceed with an overview of how TestCafe competes with Selenium.

Comparing TestCafe and Selenium

TestCafe, with its 8,000+ stars on GitHub, is gaining a reputation as the 'next big thing' in the test automation world. Let's compare this new challenger with Selenium – a heavyweight leader with almost 18k+ stars that has ruled the industry for more than 15 years.

To start automating with Selenium, you will have to install the WebDriver client for the desired programming language and corresponding drivers for each browser you want your tests to run at. This may sound like an easy thing to do, but it's quite a time-consuming task to just get started with testing and is far from the ideal scenario of the run-one-command simplicity that we're used to with the majority of the packages in the Node.js infrastructure.

TestCafe includes a number of features that would not be possible if TestCafe was built on top of Selenium, such as spawning isolated test environments. Each of the tests performed by TestCafe runs as if it was started in a new incognito tab, so all the cookies and the storage are purged. This helps to reduce test code duplication and gives a significant execution time economy as you don't need to clear the browser state between tests to make them independent of each other.

This also enables one more extremely useful feature – user roles, that lets you save the state of different logged-in users and switch between them any time in any test (`https://devexpress.github.io/testcafe/documentation/guides/advanced-guides/authentication.html`).

Built-in automatic waiting is yet another killer feature introduced in TestCafe. What it means is that TestCafe will automatically wait for all XHR requests and page loads to be finished before running each test action, so you no longer need to write custom waiters in your code.

Let's compare TestCafe and Selenium side by side:

Feature	TestCafe	Selenium
Initial release year	2016	2004
Average version release	Every 9 days	Every 2 months
License type	MIT	Apache License 2.0
Written in	JavaScript	Java
Supported programming languages	JavaScript, TypeScript and CoffeeScript	C#, Groovy, Java, Perl, PHP, Python, Ruby, Kotlin and Scala
Major operating systems support	Yes	Yes
Major browsers support	Yes	Yes
Browser provider plugins (SauceLabs and BrowserStack)	Yes	Yes
Set up in 15 minutes	Yes	No
Headless testing	Yes	No
Built-in auto waits	Yes	No
Built-in assertions	Yes	No
Built-in concurrent execution	Yes	No
Built-in XPath selectors support	No	Yes
Framework specific selectors (React, Angular, and Vue)	Yes	No
User roles	Yes	No
User interface for debugging	Yes	No
Compatibility issues due to webdrivers developed by different browser vendors	No	Yes

Figure 1.0 - Table comparing TestCafe and Selenium

To sum up what we have just learned, Selenium definitely provides an advantage with the number of supported programming languages, but needs a lot of tweaking and extending to work properly. On the other hand, TestCafe only supports JavaScript, TypeScript and CoffeeScript but offers much more comfort and ease of usage right out of the box.

Let's proceed with our exploration and shed some light on the test project that we will be developing throughout the following chapters.

Reviewing the test project we will build

As we have got acquainted with the main features of TestCafe, let's think about the best way we can leverage this testing framework for our practical needs.

To make a set of tests that are reusable and demonstrate the main concepts of TestCafe, we will need an application that can be tested. It should be accessible online and should have a number of standard features, such as logging in, logging out, creating a new entity, displaying an entity, updating an entity, and deleting an entity.

The application we will use to do this is Redmine.

Selecting a test application

All of the previously mentioned features are present in any bug tracking system. However, one of the few applications that is publicly available and free to use is Redmine (`http://demo.redmine.org/`):

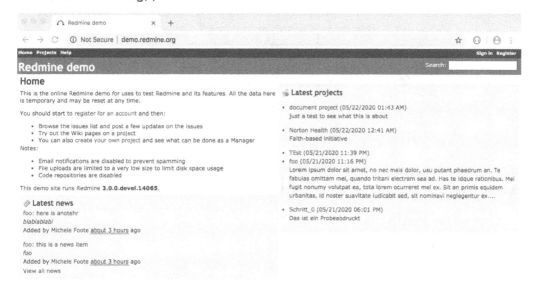

Figure 1.1 – Redmine demo web portal

Redmine is a web-based project management and issue-tracking tool released on June 25, 2006 and was written in Ruby on Rails. It is open sourced under the terms of the **GNU General Public License (GPL) v2**. Some of the features that Redmine supports include issue management (create, read, update, and delete), version management, document management, news, files, directories, calendars, charts, roadmaps, activity view, and member roles and permission management.

That's an impressive list, isn't it? Also, it is cross-platform, cross-database, and supports 49 languages. Redmine perfectly combines issue tracking and project management functionality, and can be considered a leading project management solution in the open source world.

Writing test cases

As we now have a web application for testing, let's get familiar with it and write some test cases. We don't have to execute these tests right now, but we will need them when writing automated tests later on in the book.

Here is what the Redmine login page looks like:

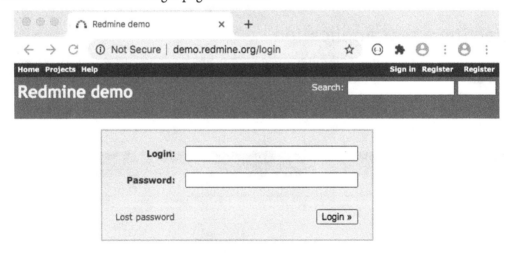

Figure 1.2 – Redmine login page

Let's break down the actions that we'll need to perform for logging in:

1.   Click on the **Sign in** link.

2.   Type in the login details for the **Login** input.

3.   Type in the password for the **Password** input.

4.   Click on the **Login** button.

Here is what we'll see after logging in successfully:

Figure 1.3 – The Redmine logged-in page

To confirm that you have logged in properly, check whether the username is displayed in the top-right corner of the page. That's it – our first test case is ready!

But even before logging in, we will need to create a new test user. We will be doing this for each new test run – that's OK, however, as all users are wiped out from the Redmine demo portal on a regular basis. To stay on the safe side, for the test user's email, we will use one of the temporary email services – `test_user_testcafe_poc{randomDigits}@sharklasers.com` – and password – `test_user_testcafe_poc`.

To continue writing test cases in a more structured way, let's break them down into blocks one by one.

Creating a new user

Follow these steps to create a new user:

1. Click on the **Register** link.
2. Fill in the **Login** field.
3. Fill in the **Password** field.
4. Fill in the **Confirmation** field.
5. Fill in the **First name** field.
6. Fill in the **Last name** field.
7. Fill in the **Email** field.
8. Click on the **Submit** button.

The expected result is the **Your account has been activated. You can now log in.** notification, which should be displayed as follows:

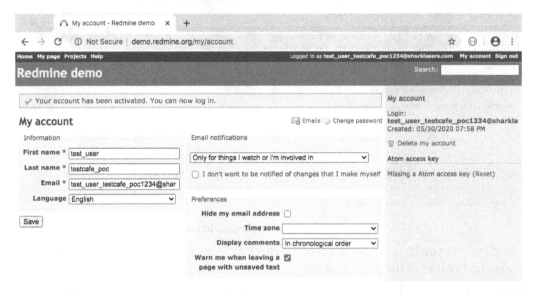

Figure 1.4 – Account activated

Logging in

Follow these steps to log in:

1. Click on the **Sign in** link.
2. Fill in the **Login** field.
3. Fill in the **Password** field.
4. Click on the **Login** button.

The expected result is that the username should be displayed in the top-right corner of the page:

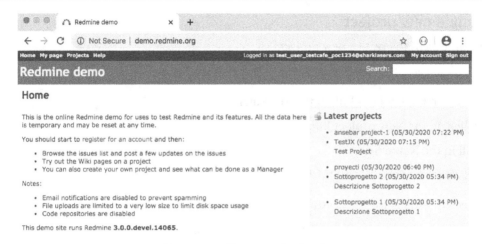

Figure 1.5 – Username displayed

Logging out

Follow these steps to log out:

1. Log in.

2. Click on the **Sign out** button.

The expected result is that the sign-in link should be displayed in the top-right corner of the page:

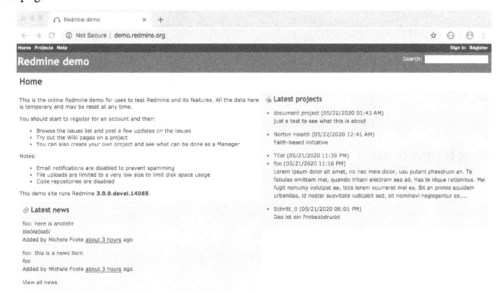

Figure 1.6 – Sign-in link displayed

Creating a new project

Follow these steps to create a new project:

1. Log in.

2. Click on the **Projects** link in the top panel.

3. Click on the **New project** link.

4. Fill in the **Name** field.

5. Click on the **Create** button.

The expected result is the **Successful creation.** notification displayed at the top:

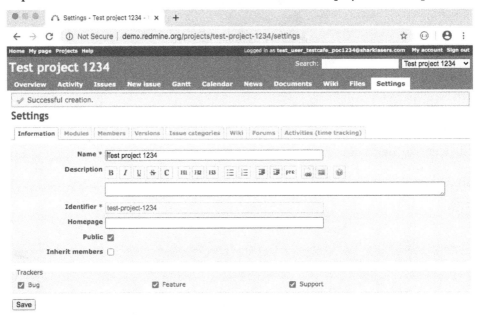

Figure 1.7 – The Successful creation. notification displayed

Creating a new issue

Follow these steps to create a new issue:

1. Log in.

2. Click on the **Projects** link in the top panel.

3. Click on the project link.

4. Click on the **New issue** link.

5. Fill in the **Subject** field.

6. Fill in the **Description** field.

7. Set **Priority** to **High**.

8. Click on the **Create** button.

The expected result is that the **Issue created.** notification should be displayed:

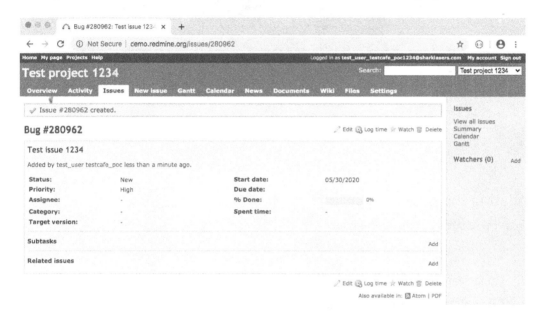

Figure 1.8 – The Issue created. notification displayed

Verifying that the issue is displayed on a project page

Follow these steps to verify that the issue is displayed on a project page:

1. Log in.

2. Create a new issue.

3. Click on the **Projects** link in the top panel.

4. Click on the project link.

5. Click on the **Issues** link.

The expected result is that the issue link should be displayed:

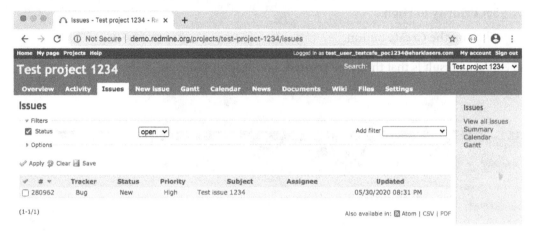

Figure 1.9 – Issue link displayed

Updating the issue

Follow these steps to update the issue:

1. Log in.

2. Create a new issue.

3. Click on the **Projects** link in the top panel.

4. Click on the project link.

5. Click on the **Issues** link.

6. Click on the issue link.

7. Click on the **Edit** link.

8. Clear the **Subject** field and fill it in with a new subject.

9. Set **Priority** to **Normal**.

10. Click on the **Submit** button.

The expected result is that the **Successful update.** notification should be displayed:

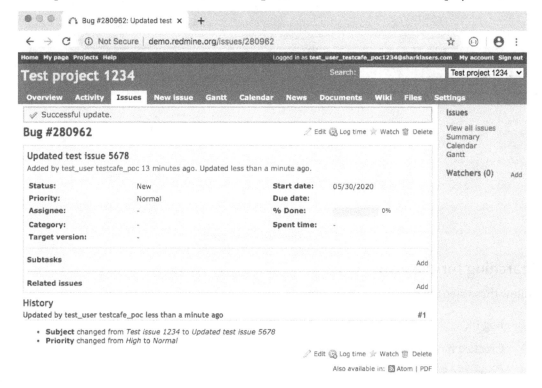

Figure 1.10 – The Successful update. notification displayed

Verifying that the updated issue is displayed on a project page

Follow these steps to verify that the updated issue is displayed on a project page:

1. Log in.
2. Create a new issue.
3. Click on the **Projects** link in the top panel.
4. Click on the project link.
5. Click on the **Issues** link.

The expected result is that the updated issue link should be displayed:

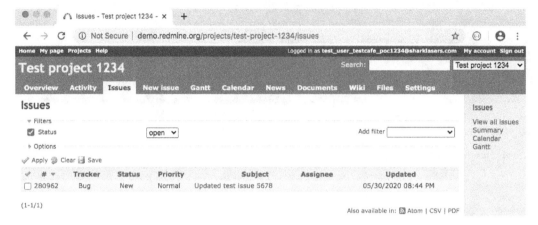

Figure 1.11 – Updated issue link displayed

Searching for the issue

Follow these steps to search for the issue:

1. Log in.

2. Create a new issue.

3. Open the **Search** page.

4. Type the issue's subject into the **Search** field.

5. Click on the **Submit** button.

The expected result is that the issue link should be displayed:

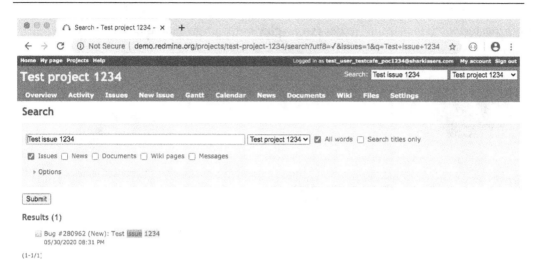

Figure 1.12 – Issue link displayed

Deleting the issue

Follow these steps to delete the issue:

1. Log in.

2. Create a new issue.

3. Click on the **Projects** link in the top panel.

4. Click on the project link.

5. Click on the **Issues** link.

6. Click on the issue link.

7. Click on the **Delete** link.

8. Confirm the deletion in the browser modal window.

The expected result is that the **No data to display** notification should be displayed:

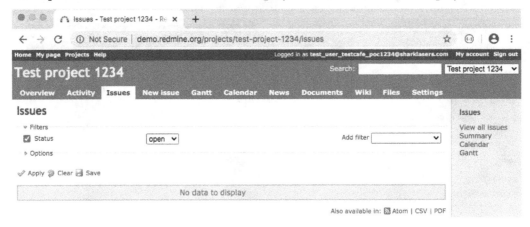

Figure 1.13 – The No data to display notification displayed

Uploading a file

Follow these steps to upload a file:

1. Log in.
2. Click on the **Projects** link in the top panel.
3. Click on the project link.
4. Click on the **Files** link.
5. Click on the **New** file link.
6. Set the path to a file.
7. Click on the **Add** button.

The expected result is that a link to the file and the MD5 checksum should be displayed:

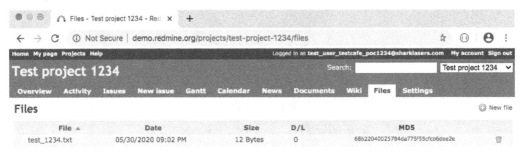

Figure 1.14 – Link to the file and the MD5 checksum displayed

Deleting the file

Follow these steps to delete the file:

1. Log in.

2. Upload a new file.

3. Click on the **Projects** link in the top panel.

4. Click on the project link.

5. Click on the **Files** link.

6. Click on the trash bin icon.

7. Confirm the deletion in the browser modal window.

The expected result is that a link to the file and the MD5 checksum should not be displayed:

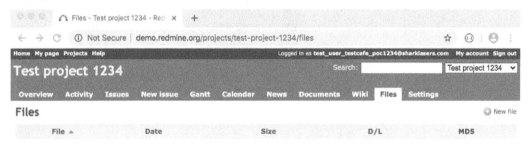

Figure 1.15 – Link to the file and MD5 checksum not displayed

While this test suite is relatively simple to build, it allows showcasing some of the most prominent features of TestCafe. Additionally, it demonstrates running the tests against a free and simple-to-use website, and it does not require you to build and deploy you own servers or backend services.

Summary

In this chapter, we reviewed what TestCafe is and its main features. While comparing TestCafe with its old and canonical rival – Selenium – we observed the strong and weak points of both frameworks. The main difference between Selenium and TestCafe is that Selenium is more heavyweight as it runs code through the Selenium server by interacting with the browser process itself, whereas TestCafe inserts a proxy in between that rewrites each URL and injects the test scripts into the browser. It runs as a Node.js process and can perform operations in both Node.js and browser contexts. The primary goal of TestCafe is to provide a modern tool that mitigates main test automation pain points and provides a convenient way to set up, maintain, and create new tests.

We also went through the testing project and came up with a plan for what test cases should be covered with the upcoming automation.

In the next chapter, we will dive deeper and see how TestCafe operates under the hood, including what API it has and how built-in wait functions can help us to transform our test cases into a fast and reliable suite of automated tests.

2
Exploring TestCafe Under the Hood

The main goal of this chapter is to learn how TestCafe works under the hood and how it can be used in **test automation** to cover different features of websites and portals. We will get acquainted with the architecture of TestCafe, its API, and custom client-side code.

These topics will give us the ability to understand what main methods and functions of TestCafe are available out of the box and how to invoke them.

In this chapter, we're going to cover the following main topics:

- Scouting the TestCafe architecture.
- Learning about the TestCafe API.
- Executing custom client-side code.

Scouting the TestCafe architecture

From the beginning of time, end-to-end web testing frameworks have depended on external drivers to emulate user actions in real browsers. This approach, however, has a number of downsides:

- **Third-party dependencies and a limited number of supported browsers**: You had to download, install, configure, and update additional drivers or libraries for each test environment (and sometimes even for each test run). In addition to that, you could only use the browsers supported by each driver.

- **Lack of flexibility**: Old tools were unable to operate on the tested page directly. As long as the test code does not interfere with the app code, operating on the tested page directly enables the tool to execute many additional scenarios and workarounds. For example, this way it can add and remove styles or change the visibility of any elements on the tested page.

- **Code duplication**: Legacy testing frameworks ran with the same browser instance during the entire test run, maintaining the tested web application state from test to test (and keeping the same values in cookies and storage). As a consequence, end-to-end tests had a huge amount of duplicated code for clearing the web application state between tests to avoid interference.

However, TestCafe has a fix for each of these problems.

The core idea behind the architecture of TestCafe is that users should not need any external drivers to run end-to-end browser tests. Instead, all the test scripts that emulate user actions can be executed from the page itself. This enables a true cross-platform and cross-browser approach as tests will be able to run on any device with a modern browser!

After each test finishes its execution, TestCafe purges the browser state: it deletes cookies, clears `localStorage` and `sessionStorage`, and reloads the page. If you launch several tests in parallel, TestCafe executes each test run in an independent server-side context to prevent server-side collisions.

TestCafe execution can be split into two parts:

- Server-side (in the Node.js process).
- Client-side (in the browser).

Let's take a look at each of these parts.

The server side

Test code is performed in the Node.js environment on the **server side**. This enables TestCafe to use advantages of standalone server-side code, including the possibility of launching tested web application servers before tests and enhanced control over the testing environment and test execution.

Executing test code in Node.js provides a lot of advantages:

- Database preparation and the launching of the application can be done from within the tests.

- Tests have access to the server's filesystem, so you can read data or create files needed for testing.

- Tests can use all recent syntax features of Node.js. In addition to that, you can include and utilize any Node.js third-party packages.

- Improved stability and speed of execution due to test logic separation from automation scripts.

Since Node.js code executes on the server, it doesn't have direct access to the **Document Object Model (DOM)** of the page or browser API, but this is handled by custom client-side functions that have access to the DOM and are executed in the browser context.

The client side

TestCafe automation scripts are designed to imitate user actions on any tested page. Their main goal is to enable you to write high-level cross-browser tests, so element-focusing, triggering events, and processing attributes are performed in the same way as a real human would in a browser.

Scripts that emulate user activity (TestCafe internal scripts) run on the **client side** on the tested page in the browser. This enables TestCafe to utilize the advantages of browser scripts, including built-in smart waits, mobile testing, and user roles. For client-side code to work in the browser, TestCafe proxies the tested page on the server and injects the scripts into its code. This approach is also known as a reverse proxy. When you run TestCafe tests, the browser address bar shows a URL that is prefixed with some digits – this is because TestCafe uses its own open source URL-rewriting proxy (`https://github.com/DevExpress/testcafe-hammerhead`) and proxies the tested pages.

When you run tests with TestCafe, a reverse proxy is automatically launched locally on your computer. It injects automation scripts into the tested page, so neither the page code nor the resources it communicates with can tell that the page has been modified. In other words, when TestCafe proxies the tested page, it adds automation scripts and rewrites all the URLs on the tested page to point to the proxy:

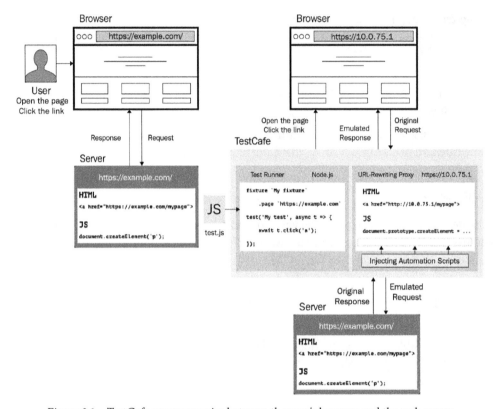

Figure 2.1 – TestCafe reverse proxies between the user's browser and the web server

When the browser refers to these new, rewritten URLs, the original resources are also proxied and enhanced in the same way. TestCafe also mocks the browser API to separate automation scripts from the rest of the page code. The proxying mechanism is absolutely safe – it guarantees that the page appears to be hosted at the original URL, even to the test code.

In this section, we reviewed how TestCafe operates from the server and client sides. We also learned about the main advantages of this architecture, including the possibility to prelaunch applications before tests, extend control over testing environments, proxying and injecting scripts, which enables smart waiting, mobile testing, and user roles, which we will discuss a bit later.

TestCafe supports JavaScript – the most popular programming language for web development – which allows most users to use their existing coding skills and minimizes the learning curve for newcomers. In addition to that, its clear API makes tests easy to create, read, and maintain. So, let's see what methods TestCafe has to offer.

Learning about the TestCafe API

Since the server-side code runs in Node.js, tests should be written in JavaScript (TypeScript and CoffeeScript are also supported, but eventually, everything should be transpiled into JavaScript).

TestCafe utilizes a minimalistic API that provides less than a few dozen methods, which are then transformed into user actions on the page. As our tests will be using the TestCafe API methods to interact with the pages, let's review the main interaction groups supported in TestCafe:

- Elements selection.
- Actions.
- Assertions.
- User roles.

Let's discover each of these interactions in more detail.

Elements selection

TestCafe utilizes an advanced mechanism with built-in waiting to locate target elements for an action or assertion. To perform an action (such as click, hover, type, and so on) or to make an assertion, you should first identify the target page element. This is as easy as specifying a standard CSS selector. For more complex situations, you can chain methods (such as, for example, getting an element by class name, then getting its second child, and then finally, getting its third sibling). Selector strings should be passed inside chainable `Selector` constructors to create a selector.

For example, you can click on a button with the `button-test` class, as follows:

```
const { Selector } = require('testcafe');

const buttonTest = Selector('.button-test');
```

For more complex situations, you can traverse the DOM tree by chaining selectors:

```
const { Selector } = require('testcafe');

const linkTest = Selector('#block-test')
    .child('a')
    .withAttribute('href', 'https://test-site.com/main.html')
    .withText('Second link');
```

What this chain of selectors does is the following:

1. Selects an element with the `block-test` id.

2. Selects its child elements.

3. Filters them by the a tag.

4. Selects elements with the `href` attribute that includes `https://test-site.com/main.html`.

5. Selects elements that include the `Second link` text.

> **Note**
>
> If a selector matches several elements, the subsequent methods return results for all the elements that were matched.

TestCafe provides a number of methods that search for elements relative to the selected element (keep in mind that all of these methods should be prepended with `Selector(cssSelector)`). Most of these methods accept `index` as an argument, which should be a zero-based number (0 will be the closest relative element in the set). If the number is negative, the index is counted from the end of the matched set. Here are the methods:

- `.find(cssSelector)`: Finds the descendant nodes of all the nodes in the matched set and uses a CSS selector to filter them (the CSS selector should be a string) (`https://devexpress.github.io/testcafe/documentation/reference/test-api/selector/find.html`).

- `.parent(index)`: Finds the parents of all the nodes in the matched set (the first element in the set is the closest parent) (`https://devexpress.github.io/testcafe/documentation/reference/test-api/selector/parent.html`).

- `.child(index)`: Finds the child elements of all nodes in the matched set (https://devexpress.github.io/testcafe/documentation/reference/test-api/selector/child.html).

- `.sibling(index)`: Finds the sibling elements of all the nodes in the matched set (https://devexpress.github.io/testcafe/documentation/reference/test-api/selector/sibling.html).

- `.nextSibling(index)`: Finds the succeeding sibling elements of all the nodes in the matched set (https://devexpress.github.io/testcafe/documentation/reference/test-api/selector/nextsibling.html).

- `.prevSibling(index)`: Finds the preceding sibling elements of all nodes in the matched set and filters them by index (https://devexpress.github.io/testcafe/documentation/reference/test-api/selector/prevsibling.html).

Now, let's look at the methods that filter elements from the selector. The same as before, all of these methods should be prepended with `Selector(cssSelector)`. Here are the methods:

- `.nth(index)`: Selects an element with the specified index in the matched set. Here, the `index` argument should be a zero-based number (0 will be the closest relative element in the set). If it is negative, the index is counted from the end of the matched set (https://devexpress.github.io/testcafe/documentation/reference/test-api/selector/nth.html).

- `.withText(text)`: Selects elements that contain the specified text. Here, `text` is the element's text content (the `text` argument is a case-sensitive string) or a **regular expression (RegExp)** that should match the element's text (https://devexpress.github.io/testcafe/documentation/reference/test-api/selector/withtext.html).

- `.withExactText(text)`: Selects elements whose text content strictly matches the specified text. Here, `text` is the element's text content (the `text` argument is a case-sensitive string) (https://devexpress.github.io/testcafe/documentation/reference/test-api/selector/withexacttext.html).

- `.withAttribute(attrName[, attrValue])`: Selects elements that contain the specified attribute. Here, `attrName` can be a case-sensitive string or a `RegExp`, and optionally, `attrValue` can also be a case-sensitive string or a `RegExp` (https://devexpress.github.io/ testcafe/documentation/reference/test-api/selector/ withattribute.html).

- `.filterVisible()`: Selects elements that do not have the `display:` `none;` or `visibility: hidden;` CSS properties and have non-zero widths and heights (https://devexpress.github.io/testcafe/documentation/ reference/test-api/selector/filtervisible.html).

- `.filterHidden()`: Selects elements that have the `display:` `none;` or `visibility: hidden;` CSS properties, or zero widths or heights (https://devexpress.github.io/testcafe/documentation/ reference/test-api/selector/filterhidden.html).

- `.filter(cssSelector)`: Selects elements that match the CSS selector (the CSS selector should be a string used to filter child elements). Also, instead of the `cssSelector` argument, you could provide `filterFn` (a function predicate used to filter the elements) and, optionally, `dependencies` (an object with functions, variables, or objects passed to the `filterFn` function) (https://devexpress. github.io/testcafe/documentation/reference/test-api/ selector/filter.html).

When a selector is executed, TestCafe will be waiting for the target node to appear on the page until the selector timeout expires. You can specify the timeout (in milliseconds) in the following cases:

- **Before test launch**: It can be specified for all elements with the `selectorTimeout` config option in the `.testcaferc.json` configuration file (https://devexpress.github.io/testcafe/documentation/ reference/configuration-file.html).

- **During test launch**: It can be set for all elements with the `--selector-timeout` command-line option (https://devexpress.github.io/testcafe/ documentation/reference/command-line-interface.html#-- selector-timeout-ms).

- **In test code**: It can be set as an additional option inside `Selector` (https:// devexpress.github.io/testcafe/documentation/reference/ test-api/selector/constructor.html#optionstimeout) to set the timeout for any particular element.

During the timeout, the selector is rerun until it returns a DOM element or the timeout is surpassed. If TestCafe can't find the corresponding node in the DOM, the test is marked as failed.

Actions

The TestCafe API provides a set of action methods to interact with the page (such as click, type, select text, hover, and so on). You can call them one after another in a chained fashion. All of these methods should be prepended with t as they are the methods of the test controller object (https://devexpress.github.io/testcafe/documentation/reference/test-api/testcontroller/). Also, selector can be a string, selector, DOM node, function, or Promise; and optionally, you can use options, which is an object with a set of options containing supplementary parameters for the action (unless otherwise specified). Here are all the main action methods:

- .click(selector[, options]): Clicks on an element on a page (https://devexpress.github.io/testcafe/documentation/reference/test-api/testcontroller/click.html).

- .doubleClick(selector[, options]): Double-clicks on an element on a page (https://devexpress.github.io/testcafe/documentation/reference/test-api/testcontroller/doubleclick.html).

- .rightClick(selector[, options]): Right-clicks on an element on a page (https://devexpress.github.io/testcafe/documentation/reference/test-api/testcontroller/rightclick.html).

- .pressKey(keys[, options]): Presses the specified keyboard keys. Here, keys is a sequence of keys and key combinations to be pressed (https://devexpress.github.io/testcafe/documentation/reference/test-api/testcontroller/presskey.html).

- .navigateTo(url): Navigates to the specified URL. Here, url is a string with the URL to navigate to (which can be absolute or relative to the current page) (https://devexpress.github.io/testcafe/documentation/reference/test-api/testcontroller/navigateto.html).

- .typeText(selector, text[, options]): Types the specified text into an input element. Here, text is a string of the text to be typed into the specified web page element (https://devexpress.github.io/testcafe/documentation/reference/test-api/testcontroller/typetext.html).

- `.selectText(selector[, startPos][, endPos][, options])`:
  Selects text in input elements of various types. Here, `startPos` is the number
  (zero-based integer, 0 by default) of the start position of the selection. Optionally,
  `endPos` is the number (zero-based integer; by default, it is equal to the length
  of the visible text content) of the end position of the selection (`https://`
  `devexpress.github.io/testcafe/documentation/reference/`
  `test-api/testcontroller/selecttext.html`).

- `.hover(selector[, options])`: Hovers the mouse pointer over a web page
  element (`https://devexpress.github.io/testcafe/documentation/`
  `reference/test-api/testcontroller/hover.html`).

- `.drag(selector, dragOffsetX, dragOffsetY[, options])`: Drags
  an element to a specified offset. Here, `dragOffsetX` is the number of pixels for
  the X offset (horizontal) of the drop coordinates from the original position of the
  mouse pointer, and `dragOffsetY` is the number of pixels for the Y offset (vertical)
  of the drop coordinates from the original position of the mouse pointer (`https://`
  `devexpress.github.io/testcafe/documentation/reference/`
  `test-api/testcontroller/drag.html`).

- `.dragToElement(selector, destinationSelector[, options])`:
  Drags an element onto another web page element. Here, `destinationSelector`
  should identify the web element that will be the drop location (`https://`
  `devexpress.github.io/testcafe/documentation/reference/`
  `test-api/testcontroller/dragtoelement.html`).

- `.setFilesToUpload(selector, filePath)`: Adds file paths to the
  specified file upload input. Here, `filePath` is a string or an array with the path
  to the uploaded file (or several paths, in the case of an array). Relative paths
  are resolved against the folder with the test file (`https://devexpress.`
  `github.io/testcafe/documentation/reference/test-api/`
  `testcontroller/setfilestoupload.html`).

- `.clearUpload(selector)`: Deletes all the file paths from the specified
  file upload input (`https://devexpress.github.io/testcafe/`
  `documentation/reference/test-api/testcontroller/`
  `clearupload.html`).

- `.takeScreenshot([options])`: Takes a screenshot of the entire page. The optional `options` object can include the following properties: the `path` string with the screenshot file's relative path and name or a `fullPage` boolean (false by default) that specifies if the full page should be captured, including content that is not visible due to overflow (https://devexpress.github.io/testcafe/documentation/reference/test-api/testcontroller/takescreenshot.html).

- `.takeElementScreenshot(selector[, path][, options])`: Takes a screenshot of the specified web page element. Here, `path` (an optional argument) is a string with the screenshot file's relative path and name (https://devexpress.github.io/testcafe/documentation/reference/test-api/testcontroller/takeelementscreenshot.html).

- `.switchToIframe(selector)`: Switches the browsing context of the test to the specified `<iframe>` (https://devexpress.github.io/testcafe/documentation/reference/test-api/testcontroller/switchtoiframe.html).

- `.switchToMainWindow()`: Switches the browsing context of the test from an `<iframe>` back to the main window (https://devexpress.github.io/testcafe/documentation/reference/test-api/testcontroller/switchtomainwindow.html).

- `.setNativeDialogHandler(fn(type, text, url)[, options])`: Specifies a handler function to deal with native dialogs triggered during the test run. Here, `fn(type, text, url)` can be a function or a client function that will be invoked whenever a native dialog is triggered (`null` to delete the native dialog handler). The handler function can utilize three arguments: `type`, which is a string with the type of the native dialog (`confirm`, `alert`, `prompt`, or `beforeunload`); `text`, which is a string with the dialog message text; and `url`, which is a string with the URL of the page that triggered the dialog (used to check whether the dialog was called from the main window or an `<iframe>`) (https://devexpress.github.io/testcafe/documentation/reference/test-api/testcontroller/setnativedialoghandler.html).

- `.getNativeDialogHistory()`: Provides a history of the native dialogs that were triggered (https://devexpress.github.io/testcafe/documentation/reference/test-api/testcontroller/getnativedialoghistory.html).

- `.resizeWindow(width, height)`: Resizes a window to fit the provided width and height, where `width` is the value of the new width (in pixels) and `height` is the value of the new height (in pixels) (`https://devexpress.github.io/testcafe/documentation/reference/test-api/testcontroller/resizewindow.html`).

- `.resizeWindowToFitDevice(deviceName[, options])`: Resizes the window to fit the screen of the specified mobile device, where `deviceName` is a string with the device name (`https://devexpress.github.io/testcafe/documentation/reference/test-api/testcontroller/resizewindowtofitdevice.html`).

- `.maximizeWindow()`: Maximizes the browser window (`https://devexpress.github.io/testcafe/documentation/reference/test-api/testcontroller/maximizewindow.html`).

- `.wait(timeout)`: Pauses a test execution for a specified period of time. Here, `timeout` is the length of the pause duration (in milliseconds) (`https://devexpress.github.io/testcafe/documentation/reference/test-api/testcontroller/wait.html`).

Assertions

TestCafe allows you to verify elements, page properties, and parameters (equals, contains, greater, match, and so on). To write assertions, use the test controller's `t.expect` method, followed by an assertion method that accepts an expected value and optional arguments; `message` is the assertion message string that shows up in the report if the test fails and `options` is an object with a set of options containing supplementary parameters for the assertion. Here are all the assertion methods available in TestCafe out of the box:

- `.expect(actual).eql(expected[, message][, options])`: Verifies that the `actual` value is equal to the `expected` value. Here, `actual` is any type of comparison value and `expected` is any type of expected value (`https://devexpress.github.io/testcafe/documentation/reference/test-api/testcontroller/expect/eql.html`).

- `.expect(actual).notEql(expected[, message][, options])`: Verifies that the `actual` value does not equal the `expected` value. Here, `actual` is any type of comparison value and `expected` is any type of value that is expected not to be equal to `actual` (`https://devexpress.github.io/testcafe/documentation/reference/test-api/testcontroller/expect/noteql.html`).

- `.expect(actual).ok([message][, options])`: Verifies that the actual value is `true`. Here, `actual` is any type of value tested in the assertion (the assertion will pass if the actual value is `true`) (`https://devexpress.github.io/testcafe/documentation/reference/test-api/testcontroller/expect/ok.html`).

- `.expect(actual).notOk([message][, options])`: Verifies that the actual value is `false`. Here, `actual` is any type of value tested in the assertion (the assertion will pass if the actual value is `false`) (`https://devexpress.github.io/testcafe/documentation/reference/test-api/testcontroller/expect/notok.html`).

- `.expect(actual).contains(expected[, message][, options])`: Verifies that the `actual` value contains the `expected` value. Here, `actual` is any type of comparison value and `expected` is any type of expected value (the assertion will pass if the actual value contains the expected value) (`https://devexpress.github.io/testcafe/documentation/reference/test-api/testcontroller/expect/contains.html`).

- `.expect(actual).notContains(expected[, message][, options])`: Verifies that the `actual` value contains the `expected` value. Here, `actual` is any type of comparison value, and `expected` is any type of expected value (the assertion will pass if the actual value does not contain the expected value) (`https://devexpress.github.io/testcafe/documentation/reference/test-api/testcontroller/expect/notcontains.html`).

- `.expect(actual).typeOf(typeName[, message][, options])`: Asserts that the `actual` value type is `typeName`. Here, `actual` is any type of comparison value and `typeName` is a string of the expected type of an actual value (`https://devexpress.github.io/testcafe/documentation/reference/test-api/testcontroller/expect/typeof.html`).

- `.expect(actual).notTypeOf(typeName[, message][, options])`: Asserts that the `actual` value type is not `typeName`. Here, `actual` is any type of comparison value and `typeName` is a string of the type of the actual value that causes an assertion to fail (`https://devexpress.github.io/testcafe/documentation/reference/test-api/testcontroller/expect/nottypeof.html`).

- `.expect(actual).gt(expected[, message] [, options])`: Verifies that the `actual` value is greater than the `expected` value. Here, `actual` is the number tested in the assertion (the assertion will pass if the actual value is greater than the expected value) and `expected` is any type of expected value (https://devexpress.github.io/testcafe/documentation/reference/test-api/testcontroller/expect/gt.html).

- `.expect(actual).gte(expected[, message] [, options])`: Verifies that the `actual` value is greater than or equal to the `expected` value. Here, `actual` is a number tested in the assertion (the assertion will pass if the actual value is greater than or equal to the expected value), and `expected` is any type of expected value (https://devexpress.github.io/testcafe/documentation/reference/test-api/testcontroller/expect/gte.html).

- `.expect(actual).lt(expected[, message] [, options])`: Verifies that the `actual` value is less than the `expected` value. Here, `actual` is the number tested in the assertion (the assertion will pass if the actual value is less than the expected value) and `expected` is any type of expected value (https://devexpress.github.io/testcafe/documentation/reference/test-api/testcontroller/expect/lt.html).

- `.expect(actual).lte(expected[, message] [, options])`: Verifies that the `actual` value is less than or equal to the `expected` value. Here, `actual` is the number tested in the assertion (the assertion will pass if the actual value is less than or equal to the expected value) and `expected` is any type of expected value (https://devexpress.github.io/testcafe/documentation/reference/test-api/testcontroller/expect/lte.html).

- `.expect(actual).within(start, finish[, message] [, options])`: Verifies that the `actual` value is within a specified range from start to finish (bounds are inclusive). Here, `actual` is a number, `start` is the number for the lower range (inclusive), and `finish` is the number for the upper range (inclusive) (https://devexpress.github.io/testcafe/documentation/reference/test-api/testcontroller/expect/within.html).

- `.expect(actual).notWithin(start, finish[, message] [, options])`: Verifies that the `actual` value is not within the specified range from start to finish (bounds are inclusive). Here, `actual` is a number, `start` is the number for the lower range (inclusive), and `finish` is the number for the upper range (inclusive) (https://devexpress.github.io/testcafe/documentation/reference/test-api/testcontroller/expect/notwithin.html).

- `.expect(actual).match(re[, message][, options])`: Verifies that the `actual` value matches the `re` regular expression. Here, `actual` is any type of comparison value and `re` is a regular expression that is expected to match the actual value (`https://devexpress.github.io/testcafe/documentation/reference/test-api/testcontroller/expect/match.html`).

- `.expect(actual).notMatch(re[, message][, options])`: Verifies that the `actual` value does not match the `re` regular expression. Here, `actual` is any type of comparison value and `re` is a regular expression that is expected not to match the actual value (`https://devexpress.github.io/testcafe/documentation/reference/test-api/testcontroller/expect/notmatch.html`).

User roles

TestCafe has a built-in user role mechanism that emulates user actions for logging in to a website. It also saves the logged-in state of each user in a separate role that can be reused later on in any part of your tests to switch between user accounts. This approach gives access to some unique features:

- Login actions are not duplicated upon switching to a previously used role during the same session. So, for example, if you activate a role in the `beforeEach` hook, the login actions will run only once before the first test. All further tests will just reuse the existing authentication data.

- When you switch roles, the browser automatically navigates back to the page where the switch happened, so there is no need to additionally open any URLs for a new role (this behavior can be disabled if required).

- If during a test you log in to several websites, authentication data from cookies and browser storage is saved in the active role. When switching back to this role in the same test, you will be logged in to all the websites automatically.

- An anonymous built-in role that logs you out of all accounts.

Let's have a look at a practical example of creating and using roles.

To create and initialize a role, we will need to use a `Role` constructor. Then, the login page URL and actions needed to log in should be passed to `Role`. This is shown in the following code block:

```
const { Role, Selector } = require('testcafe');

const regularUser = Role('https://test-site.com/login', async
(t) => {
```

```
    await t.typeText('.login', 'TestUser')
        .typeText('.password', 'testuserpass')
        .click('#log-in');
});

const admin = Role('https://test-site.com/login', async (t) =>
{
    await t.typeText('.login', 'TestAdmin')
        .typeText('.password', 'testadminpass')
        .click('#log-in');
});

const linkLoggedInUser = Selector('.link-logged-in-user');
const linkLoggedInAdmin = Selector('.link-logged-in-admin');

fixture('My first test Fixture').page('https://test-site.com');

test('Test login with three users', async (t) => {
    await t.useRole(regularUser)
        .expect(linkLoggedInUser.exists).ok()
        .useRole(admin)
        .expect(linkLoggedInUser.exists).notOk()
        .expect(linkLoggedInAdmin.exists).ok()
        .useRole(Role.anonymous())
        .expect(linkLoggedInUser.exists).notOk()
        .expect(linkLoggedInAdmin.exists).notOk();
});
```

After you create all the required roles, you can switch between them anytime; roles are shared across tests and fixtures. Roles can even be created in a separate file and then used in any test fixture that references (requires or imports) this file.

To sum up, in this section, we reviewed the TestCafe API and the main methods that it provides. We also learned how to select elements, conduct assertions, and utilize user roles to switch between different accounts. Now, let's take a look at how custom client-side code can be executed in TestCafe to give us even more control over the browser.

Executing custom client-side code

With TestCafe, you can create client functions that can run on the client side (in the browser) and return any serializable value. For example, you can obtain the URL of the current page, set cookies, or even manipulate any elements on the page.

In some complex scenarios, TestCafe helps you write code to be executed on the tested page. Here are several examples of tasks that can be done with custom client-side code:

- Get elements from the web page for further actions. TestCafe allows you to create selectors based on client-side code that returns DOM nodes. You can write this code in the server-side test and TestCafe will run these functions in the browser when it needs to locate an element:

```
const { Selector } = require('testcafe');

const testElement = Selector(() => {
    return document.querySelector('.test-class-name');
});

await t.click(testElement);
```

- Obtain data from a client function that returns any serializable object from the client side (including any objects that can be converted to JSON). Unlike selectors, test code can access the object this client function returns. Usually, the data obtained from client functions is used to assert different page parameters. Here is an example of getting and verifying a page URL:

```
const { ClientFunction } = require('testcafe');

const getPageUrl = ClientFunction(() => {
    return window.location.href;
});

await t.expect(getPageUrl).eql('https://test-site.com');
```

- Inject custom code into the tested page. Injected scripts can then be used to add helper functions or to mock browser API:

```
fixture('My second test Fixture')
    .page('https://test-site.com')
    .clientScripts(
        'assets/jquery-latest.js',
        'scripts/location-mock.js'
    );
```

> **Note**
> It is recommended that you avoid changing the DOM with custom client-side code. A rule of thumb is to use client-side code only to explore the page, find and return information to the server.

You can find more examples of client-side scripts and injections at the following links:

- `https://devexpress.github.io/testcafe/documentation/guides/basic-guides/obtain-client-side-info.html`.
- `https://devexpress.github.io/testcafe/documentation/guides/advanced-guides/inject-client-scripts.html`.

As we just discovered, TestCafe client functions are quite useful for different browser manipulations and getting additional data to verify in our tests.

Summary

In this chapter, we learned how TestCafe works under the hood. We got acquainted with the architecture of TestCafe, saw how it performs on client and server sides, and learned about the strategies for selecting elements, actions, assertions, roles, and custom client-side code.

All of this will be used in the upcoming chapters to write our own suite of end-to-end tests. In addition to that, you can always use this chapter as a reference to search for any particular method or assertion and see how it's called and what it does.

Now, let's move on from the main methods and functions of TestCafe to more practical aspects, such as setting up the testing environment for our future automated tests.

3
Setting Up the Environment

The main learning goal of this chapter is to get used to setting up the testing environment for writing end-to-end tests using TestCafe. You will learn how to set up a Node.js environment (including TestCafe itself), create a basic configuration file to run the tests, and structure the test code to follow the best practices.

This is especially important because in real life, each new project/repository usually requires a testing infrastructure to be set up to prevent regressions and to keep the code quality high.

To sum up, this chapter will cover the following main topics:

- Setting up the test project environment.
- Creating the test project configuration file.
- Structuring the test code.

Technical requirements

All the code examples for this chapter can be found on GitHub at `https://github.com/PacktPublishing/Modern-Web-Testing-with-TestCafe/tree/master/ch3`.

Setting up the test project environment

It is important to set up the environment properly now as we will be using it for the rest of the chapter and up to the end of this book. Doing so will also help you understand the basics of how Node.js deals with different packages and how to spin up pretty much any JavaScript/Node.js-based testing framework. We will divide the setup process into two sections:

- Installing Node.js.
- Installing TestCafe.

So, let's go through the whole process, starting from the beginning—installing Node.js.

Installing Node.js

JavaScript is a client-side programming language that mostly deals with the frontend, which means it is usually processed by the browser of each user that opens your website or web application. Node.js was developed as a JavaScript runtime environment to provide the ability to use JavaScript as a server-side backend language.

In order to launch almost any development tools written in JavaScript, you'll need to use Node.js and **Node Package Manager (npm)**. This package manager is a tool that helps you install, update, and keep your Node.js project dependencies (packages) all in one place (the `node_modules` folder).

Node.js is available for a variety of operating systems, macOS, Ubuntu/Linux, and Windows being among them. The easiest way to install Node.js and `npm` is to follow these steps:

1. Open `https://nodejs.org/en/download/`.
2. Select the **long-term support (LTS)** version.
3. Select your operating system.
4. Download the installation file and run it.

Another slightly more complex but reusable way is to install Node.js through **Node Version Manager (nvm** – `https://github.com/nvm-sh/nvm`) or n (`https://github.com/tj/n`). Version managers give you the ability to install several versions of Node.js simultaneously and switch between them whenever you like, which is quite useful during test development.

Once the installation is finished, you can check whether both Node.js and npm are working properly by opening any shell (for example, Terminal or PowerShell) and executing the following:

```
$ node -v
$ npm -v
```

That should output the version number for Node.js and npm, respectively.

Installing TestCafe

As we already have Node.js and npm installed, let's proceed with installing TestCafe. It can be installed from npm locally (to run from your project folder) or globally (to run from any location).

Installing TestCafe locally

To install TestCafe locally to your project directory and save it to the dependencies list, open any shell, go to your project folder, and execute the following two commands:

```
$ npm init --yes
$ npm install testcafe --save-dev
```

The first command will create a simple `package.json` file to store all the dependencies. The second command will install the `testcafe` package and save it to the list of your project's dependencies in `package.json`.

Installing TestCafe globally

To install TestCafe globally, open any shell and execute the following command:

```
$ npm install testcafe --global
```

This will install TestCafe globally, and it will be accessible from any folder.

You can always check the version of the `testcafe` package that is installed by executing the following command:

```
$ npx testcafe -v --no-install
```

> **Note**
>
> On macOS (starting from v10.15 Catalina and up), TestCafe requires screen recording permission to carry out test actions and take screenshots and videos. When TestCafe tests launch for the first time, macOS will ask you to allow screen recording for TestCafe browser tools. Go to **System Preferences - Security and Privacy - Privacy** and check **TestCafe Browser Tools** to grant permission. When you update macOS or TestCafe, security permissions may be purged—in this case, the system will repeat the request. So, when the **Security and Privacy** popup opens again, just uncheck and recheck the **TestCafe Browser Tools** checkbox.

Now, as we have Node.js, npm, and TestCafe installed and ready, let's proceed with creating a configuration file for our tests.

Creating the test project configuration file

In this section, we will see how to configure TestCafe. However, before reviewing the main configuration options, let's set a convention for some coding style standards.

Accepting code styling convention

When writing code throughout this book, we will follow some simple rules, such as indenting with two spaces for `.json` files and four spaces for `.js` files. We will also use semicolons and single-quotes. Most popular code editors support a `.editorconfig` configuration file to automatically apply the rules:

```
root = true

[*]
indent_style = space
indent_size = 4
end_of_line = lf
insert_final_newline = true
charset = utf-8
trim_trailing_whitespace = true
max_line_length = 120
```

```
[*.json]
indent_size = 2
```

You can copy the basic config file that we will be using from `https://github.com/PacktPublishing/Modern-Web-Testing-with-TestCafe/blob/master/.editorconfig`.

Exploring the configuration settings

The TestCafe configuration settings are usually stored in the `.testcaferc.json` file in the root folder of your project. Let's look at the main options that can be specified:

- `browsers` is a string, or an array of strings, that sets one or more browsers to launch tests in. Browser aliases should be specified for any locally installed browsers, such as `chrome`, `firefox`, `safari`, `ie`, `edge`, or `opera` (`https://devexpress.github.io/testcafe/documentation/guides/concepts/browsers.html#locally-installed-browsers`). You can see the list of all the available browsers in your system—just open any shell and run the following command:

  ```
  $ npx testcafe --list-browsers
  ```

  To run tests in Chrome only, `.testcaferc.json` will look like this:

  ```
  {
      "browsers": "chrome"
  }
  ```

  To run tests in Firefox and Chrome, your test will look like this:

  ```
  {
      "browsers": ["firefox", "chrome"]
  }
  ```

  To run tests in remote browsers (such as SauceLabs, BrowserStack, CrossBrowserTesting, and so on) with a browser provider plugin, set the browser provider name, together with the browser alias and operating system, as follows:

  ```
  {
      "browsers": "saucelabs:Chrome@83.0:Windows 10"
  }
  ```

Postfixes to browser aliases can be used to launch tests in headless mode or to apply Chrome device emulation (`https://devexpress.github.io/testcafe/documentation/guides/concepts/browsers.html#use-chromium-device-emulation`):

```
{
    "browsers": ["firefox:headless",
"chrome:emulation:device=iphone X"]
}
```

> **Note**
> TestCafe starts Chrome and Firefox with a fresh profile by default, without any extensions or profile settings. If you need to launch a browser with the current user profile, add the `:userProfile` postfix flag after the browser alias.

- `src` is a string, or an array of strings, that sets a path to files or directories from where the tests should be launched. To run tests from one file, use the following code:

```
{
    "src": "tests/login-test.js"
}
```

Global patterns can be used to parse a set of files:

```
{
    "src": ["tests/**/*.js", "utils/helpers/"]
}
```

- `reporter` is a string or an array of objects that sets the name of a built-in or custom reporter for generating test reports (`https://devexpress.github.io/testcafe/documentation/guides/concepts/reporters.html`). By default, a `spec` reporter is used. To specify any other reporters—for example, `minimal`—use the following:

```
{
    "reporter": "minimal"
}
```

Multiple reporters can be set at the same time, but only one reporter can write to the console output (standard output, or `stdout`), and all other reporters should write to the files:

```json
{
  "reporter": [
    {
      "name": "minimal"
    },
    {
      "name": "json",
      "output": "tests/reports/report.json"
    },
    {
      "name": "xunit",
      "output": "tests/reports/report.xml"
    }
  ]
}
```

You can also explore and use any of the available reporters from `https://www.npmjs.com/search?q=testcafe-reporter`.

- `screenshots` is an object that allows you to set the screenshot options. These options include `path`, which is a string for the directory where screenshots are saved; `takeOnFails`, which is a boolean for whether a screenshot should be captured whenever a test fails; `pathPattern`, which is a string for the custom pattern to create a relative path and a name for the screenshot; and `fullPage`, which is a boolean for whether a screenshot should be taken of the full page (including any content that is not visible because of the overflow):

```json
{
  "screenshots": {
    "path": "tests/screenshots/",
    "takeOnFails": true,
    "pathPattern": "${DATE}_${TIME}/test-${TEST_INDEX}/${USERAGENT}/${FILE_INDEX}.png",
    "fullPage": true
  }
}
```

> **Note**
>
> See the full list of the placeholder path patterns that can be used for screenshots and videos at `https://devexpress.github.io/testcafe/ documentation/guides/advanced-guides/screenshots- and-videos.html#path-pattern-placeholders`.

- `videoPath` is a string for the directory where videos of test runs are saved:

```
{
    "videoPath": "tests/videos/"
}
```

- `videoOptions` is an object that allows you to set the video options. These options include `failedOnly`, which is a boolean that should be set to `true` to enable recording for the failed tests only or to `false` (the default) to record all the tests; `singleFile`, which is a boolean that should be set to `true` to save the whole record in a single file or to `false` (the default) for a separate file per test; and `pathPattern`, which is a string for the custom pattern to compose the relative path and the name of the video file:

```
{
    "videoOptions": {
        "failedOnly": true,
        "singleFile": true,
        "pathPattern": "${TEST_INDEX}/${USERAGENT}/${FILE_
INDEX}.mp4"
    }
}
```

- `videoEncodingOptions` is an object that sets the video encoding options (all the `FFmpeg` library options are supported, which you can find at `https:// ffmpeg.org/ffmpeg.html#Options`). For example, let's set the frame rate and video display aspect ratio:

```
{
    "videoEncodingOptions": {
        "r": 24,
        "aspect": "16:9"
    }
}
```

- quarantineMode is a boolean to switch failed tests to quarantine mode (to rerun the unstable tests):

```
{
    "quarantineMode": true
}
```

If quarantine mode is turned on, tests run will follow the next logic:

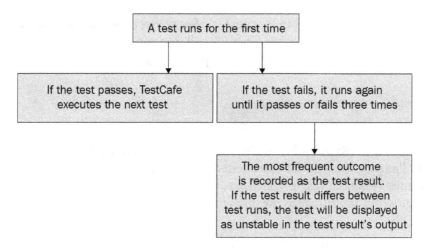

Figure 3.1 – Tests run logic in quarantine mode

- debugMode is a boolean to run tests in debugging mode:

```
{
    "debugMode": true
}
```

> **Note**
>
> If debug mode is on, test execution will be paused before the first action or assertion so that you can open the developer tools and start debugging. To make it easier, a status bar will be displayed in the footer showing the available debug actions: **Unlock page**, **Resume**, and **Next step**.

- `debugOnFail` is a boolean to automatically enable debug mode after a test fails. If this option is set to `true` (it's set to `false` by default), TestCafe will pause during the test failure so that you can view the tested page, open the developer tools, and figure out why it failed:

```
{
    "debugOnFail": true
}
```

- `skipJsErrors` is a boolean to ignore JavaScript errors on a tested web page (by default, when these errors occur, TestCafe will stop running the test and post an error message with a stack trace to the output report):

```
{
    "skipJsErrors": true
}
```

- `skipUncaughtErrors` is a boolean to ignore uncaught JavaScript errors and unhandled promise rejections on a tested web page (by default, when these errors or promise rejections occur, TestCafe will stop running the test and post an error message with a stack trace to the output report):

```
{
    "skipUncaughtErrors": true
}
```

- `appCommand` is a string to execute the specified shell command before tests are started. This option is often used to launch the application you need to run tests over (such application will be automatically stopped after all the tests are executed):

```
{
    "appCommand": "node server.js"
}
```

- `appInitDelay` is the time TestCafe will wait before launching the tests (in milliseconds; the default value is `1000`). So, this delay is used to give an application launched with the `appCommand` option some time to start:

```
{
    "appCommand": "node server.js",
    "appInitDelay": 5000
}
```

- `concurrency` is the number of browser instances spawned to run tests in parallel. TestCafe will start with a specified number of browser instances and create a pool of those instances. Tests will be launched simultaneously against this pool; each test will take the first free browser instance from the pool and run inside this instance:

```
{
    "concurrency": 4
}
```

- `selectorTimeout` is the time within which the selector sends requests to retrieve a web element node (in milliseconds; the default value is `10000`):

```
{
    "selectorTimeout": 15000
}
```

- `assertionTimeout` is the time during which TestCafe performs assertion requests (in milliseconds; the default value is `3000`). This timeout will be applied only if a selector property or a client function is used in an assertion as an `actual` value:

```
{
    "assertionTimeout": 5000
}
```

- `pageLoadTimeout` is the time after the `DOMContentLoaded` event within which TestCafe waits for the `window.load` event to be fired (in milliseconds; the default value is `3000`). TestCafe starts the test after the `window.load` event is triggered or the timeout passes (whichever happens first):

```
{
    "pageLoadTimeout": 10000
}
```

- `speed` is the test execution speed (`1` is the fastest and `0.01` is the slowest; `1` is the default). This option can be used to slow down the tests:

```
{
    "speed": 0.5
}
```

> **Note**
> If the speed is set in `.testcaferc.json` and also within the test for an individual action, the action's speed setting will have a higher priority and will override the speed set in the configuration file.

- `clientScripts` is an object, an array of objects, or a string for the scripts to be injected into any pages opened during the tests. This property is often used to add client-side mock functions, modules, or helper scripts. You can set `content`, which is a string with the code to inject the JavaScript code; `module`, which is a string with the module name to inject the module; and `path`, which is a string with the path to the file to inject the JavaScript file. Any of these settings can be paired with the optional `page` setting to set a specific page that the provided scripts should be injected into:

```
{
   "clientScripts": [
      {
         "content": "Date.prototype.getTimestamp = () => new
Date().getTime().toString();"
      },
      {
         "module": "js-automation-tools"
      },
      {
         "path": "scripts/helpers.js",
         "page": "https://test-site.com/page/"
      }
   ]
}
```

- `port1` and `port2` are numbers in the range of `0` to `65535` that represent a custom port, which TestCafe uses to launch the testing infrastructure (if ports are not set, TestCafe automatically selects them):

```
{
   "port1": 12340,
   "port2": 56789
}
```

- `hostname` is a string for the hostname of your computer, used when you run tests within remote browsers. If `hostname` is not set, TestCafe will use the operating system hostname or the network IP address of the current machine:

```
{
    "hostname": "host.test-site.com"
}
```

- `proxy` is a string for the proxy server used in your local network to access the internet:

```
{
    "proxy": "123.123.123.123:8080"
}
```

Authentication credentials can also be set with the proxy host:

```
{
    "proxy": "username:password@proxy.test-site.com"
}
```

- `proxyBypass` is a string (or an array of strings) that requires TestCafe to bypass the proxy server to access the specified resources:

```
{
    "proxyBypass": ["localhost:8080", "internal.corp.test-site.com"]
}
```

- `developmentMode` is a boolean to diagnose errors (if you want to report an issue to TestCafe Support, you should set this option to `true`):

```
{
    "developmentMode": true
}
```

- `stopOnFirstFail` is a boolean to stop a test run right after any of the tests fail:

```
{
    "stopOnFirstFail": true
}
```

- `tsConfigPath` is a string to enable TestCafe to use a custom TypeScript configuration file and set its location (`https://devexpress.github.io/testcafe/documentation/guides/concepts/typescript-and-coffeescript.html#customize-compiler-options`). A relative or an absolute path can be used:

```
{
    "tsConfigPath": "/Users/john/testcafe/tsconfig.json"
}
```

In the case of relative paths, they will be resolved against the directory from which you run TestCafe.

- `disablePageCaching` is a boolean to prevent the page's content from being cached by the browser:

```
{
    "disablePageCaching": true
}
```

When browsers open a cached page inside the role code, the `localStorage` and `sessionStorage` content will not be saved. To keep the storage items after navigation, set `disablePageCaching` to `true`.

> **Note**
>
> Here is a good example of a `.testcaferc.json` file with all the main settings: `https://github.com/DevExpress/testcafe/blob/master/examples/.testcaferc.json`.

Creating a basic configuration for the test project

Now, let's assemble all that we have learned in this section and create a folder with the basic configuration for our test project by opening any shell (for example, we will use Terminal with Bash) and executing the following steps:

1. As we have already downloaded and installed Node.js, let's check its version:

    ```
    $ node -v
    ```

2. Then, create a folder for your future test project:

    ```
    $ mkdir test-project
    ```

3. Now, go to that folder and initiate a basic package.json file to store all the dependencies:

    ```
    $ cd test-project/
    $ npm init --yes
    ```

4. After that, install the TestCafe package and save it to your list as a development dependency:

    ```
    $ npm install testcafe --save-dev
    ```

5. As a final step (for now), create a .testcaferc.json configuration file with a minimal set of options:

    ```json
    {
      "browsers": "chrome",
      "src": [
        "tests/**/*.js",
        "tests/**/*.feature"
      ],
      "screenshots": {
        "path": "tests/screenshots/",
        "takeOnFails": true,
        "pathPattern": "${DATE}_${TIME}/test-${TEST_
    INDEX}/${USERAGENT}/${FILE_INDEX}.png"
      },
      "quarantineMode": false,
      "stopOnFirstFail": true,
      "skipJsErrors": true,
    ```

```
    "skipUncaughtErrors": true,
    "concurrency": 1,
    "selectorTimeout": 3000,
    "assertionTimeout": 1000,
    "pageLoadTimeout": 1000,
    "disablePageCaching": true
}
```

We have covered the options from this file in the *Exploring the configuration settings* section, so you can always refer back to it to understand this example.

You can also review and download this configuration file from GitHub at `https://github.com/PacktPublishing/Modern-Web-Testing-with-TestCafe/blob/master/ch3/test-project/.testcaferc.json`.

As we installed Node.js and TestCafe and created a basic config file, let's continue setting up our test project by organizing our test code structure.

Structuring the test code

To gain a better understanding of test code structure organization, let's divide it into several parts: fixtures, tests, the starting web page, metadata, and skipping tests.

Fixtures

TestCafe tests are usually grouped into test suites, called fixtures (which are the same as the `describe` blocks in the Jasmine and Mocha test frameworks). Any JavaScript, TypeScript, or CoffeeScript files with TestCafe tests should contain one or more fixtures. Test fixtures can be declared with the `fixture` function, which only accepts one argument—`fixtureName`—which is a string for the name of the fixture (set of tests):

```
fixture('Name for the set of the tests');
```

Alternatively, you can write this without the brackets:

```
fixture `Name for the set of the tests`;
```

A fixture is basically a wrapper to indicate the beginning of a set of tests. Let's see how these tests should be structured.

Tests

Tests are usually written right after the `fixture` declaration. To create a test, call the `test` function, which accepts two arguments:

- `testName`: A string for the name of the test.

- `function`: An asynchronous function that contains the test code and accepts one argument — `t`, which is an object for the test controller used to access all actions and assertions.

A simple test with the block of code usually looks like this:

```
test('Go to the main page', async (t) => {
    await t.click('#button-main-page');
    await t.expect(Selector('#logo-main-page').visible).ok();
});
```

Due to the fact that TestCafe tests are executed on the server side, you can use any additional packages or modules. Also, inside the test, you can do the following:

- Use test actions to interact with the tested web page.

- Use selectors and client functions to get information regarding page element states or obtain other data from the client side.

- Use assertions to verify whether the page elements have the expected parameters.

Now, let's see how to specify a starting page for all tests in a fixture.

The starting web page

You can set the initial web page that will be the starting point for all tests in a fixture with the `fixture.page` function. It only accepts one argument—`url`, which is a string for the URL of the web page where all tests in a fixture start:

```
fixture('Contacts page').page('http://test-site.com/example');

test('Test Contact form', async (t) => {
    // Starts at http://test-site.com/example
});
```

Next, let's see how to specify metadata for fixtures and tests.

Metadata

In TestCafe, you can also provide additional information for tests, such as key-value metadata. This can be used to filter tests and display this data in reports. To define metadata, use the `fixture.meta` and `test.meta` methods. They accept two string arguments:

- `name`: A string for the name of the metadata entry.

- `value`: A string for the value of the metadata entry.

Alternatively, they can accept one argument—`metadata`, which is an object for key-value pairs of metadata.

Both styles of setting metadata can be combined, which will look like this:

```
fixture('Contacts page')
    .meta('env', 'production')
    .meta('fixtureId', 'f0001')
    .meta({ author: 'John', creationDate: '01.06.2020' });

test.meta('testId', 't0001')
    .meta({ testType: 'fast', testedFeatureVersion: '1.1' })
    ('Test Contact form', async (t) => {
    // Your test code
});
```

Fixtures or tests can be launched by the specific metadata values that they contain. To filter tests by `metadata`, add the `filter.testMeta` and `filter.fixtureMeta` properties to the `.testcaferc.json` configuration file:

```
{
  "filter": {
    "fixtureMeta": {
      "env": "production",
      "author": "John"
    },
    "testMeta": {
      "testType": "fast",
      "testedFeatureVersion": "1.1"
    }
  }
}
```

This configuration will run only tests that have the `testType` property of `metadata` set to `fast` and `testedFeatureVersion` set to `1.1`, as well as tests whose fixture's metadata has the `env` property set to `production` and the `author` property set to `John`.

You can use custom reporters (`https://devexpress.github.io/testcafe/documentation/guides/extend-testcafe/reporter-plugin.html`) to display fixture's and test's metadata in reports.

Skipping tests

In TestCafe, you can also specify a fixture or test to skip while all the other tests run. This is achieved with the `fixture.skip` and `test.skip` methods:

```
fixture.skip('Contacts page');

test('Test Contact form', async (t) => {
    // Your test code
});

test('Test Review form', async (t) => {
    // Your test code
});

fixture('About page');

test('Test Reviews block', async (t) => {
    // Your test code
});

test.skip('Test More info form', async (t) => {
    // Your test code
});

test('Test Our mission block', async (t) => {
    // Your test code
});
```

In this example, all tests from the `Contacts` page fixture will be excluded from running. The `Test More info form` test will not be executed either.

Another pair of useful methods is `fixture.only` and `test.only`. They are used to specify that only a particular fixture or test should be launched, and all others should be skipped. If several fixtures or tests are marked with `.only`, then all fixtures or tests marked with `.only` will be executed:

```
fixture.only('Contacts page');

test('Test Contact form', async (t) => {
    // Your test code
});

test('Test Review form', async (t) => {
    // Your test code
});

fixture('About page');

test('Test Reviews block', async (t) => {
    // Your test code
});

test.only('Test More info form', async (t) => {
    // Your test code
});

test('Test Our mission block', async (t) => {
    // Your test code
});
```

In this example, only the tests from the `Contacts` page fixture and the `Test More info form` test will be executed.

Summary

In this chapter, we learned how to set up the testing environment for writing end-to-end tests using TestCafe. We installed Node.js and TestCafe, reviewed the configuration options, and created a basic `.testcaferc.json` file to store them. In addition to that, we found out about several techniques to structure TestCafe code, including fixtures, tests, the starting web page, metadata, and skipping tests.

The lessons of this chapter are important as you will be going through the configuration phase for any new project that you'll start.

Now, we are well prepared and ready to proceed with utilizing this knowledge in writing TestCafe tests for our test project. We will learn how to create and debug a test, and will start building a real-life test suite right after that.

4

Building a Test Suite with TestCafe

Now, as we've been through the main concepts of TestCafe and reviewed its arsenal, let's draw a weapon and write some tests! The main goal here will be to get familiar with how to write a set of end-to-end tests (a test suite) with TestCafe. This is extremely important because the testing techniques that we will cover are universal and can be reused to write automated tests for any web project.

To sum up, this chapter will cover the following main topics:

- Creating a test.
- Debugging the tests.
- Writing the test project log in tests.
- Adding verifications to the test project.
- Adding custom code execution to the test project.
- Adding more tests.

Technical requirements

As we mentioned in *Chapter 3, Setting Up the Environment*, while writing code throughout this book, we will follow some coding conventions: indent with two spaces for `.json` files, four spaces for `.js` files, use semicolons, and use single quotes. We will also utilize JavaScript ES6+ syntax, including template strings.

All code examples for this chapter can be found on GitHub: `https://github.com/PacktPublishing/Modern-Web-Testing-with-TestCafe/blob/master/ch4`.

Creating a test

TestCafe supports tests written using JavaScript, TypeScript, or CoffeeScript with all modern features, such as arrow functions and `async`/`await`. In addition to that, TestCafe will automatically transpile TypeScript and CoffeeScript code before running tests, so you do not need to tackle it on your own.

As we agreed initially, throughout this book we will be using JavaScript to write the tests.

In continuation of our previous efforts from *Chapter 3, Setting Up the Environment*, we already have `test-project` folder with the `.testcaferc.json` configuration file in it. So, let's start by opening any shell (for example, we will use Terminal with bash) and following the next steps:

1. Go to `test-project` folder and create a folder for our tests:

```
$ cd test-project/
$ mkdir tests
```

2. Now go to that folder and create a `basic-tests.js` file:

```
$ cd tests/
$ touch basic-tests.js
```

3. Open `basic-tests.js` in a code editor (or IDE) of your choice and let's create a simple test.

4. We will start by including the `testcafe` module:

    ```
    const { Selector } = require('testcafe');
    ```

5. Then we declare a fixture using the `fixture` function:

    ```
    const { Selector } = require('testcafe');

    fixture('My first set of tests');
    ```

6. Declare the first test using the `test` function:

    ```
    const { Selector } = require('testcafe');

    fixture('My first set of tests');

    test('My first test', async (t) => {
        // Your test code
    });
    ```

7. As we selected Redmine (`http://demo.redmine.org/`) as our test project, set this URL as a starting page for all tests in the `'My first set of tests'` fixture using the `page` function:

    ```
    const { Selector } = require('testcafe');

    fixture('My first set of tests')
        .page('http://demo.redmine.org/');

    test('My first test', async (t) => {
        // Your test code
    });
    ```

> **Note**
>
> You can also review and download this file on GitHub: `https://github.com/PacktPublishing/Modern-Web-Testing-with-TestCafe/blob/master/ch4/test-project/tests/basic-tests1.js`.

As we now have an empty test structure, let's run it and inspect the output.

Running the test

We can easily run the test from a command shell by executing a single command with the target browser and file path:

```
$ npx testcafe chrome tests/basic-tests.js
```

The shell output will look like this:

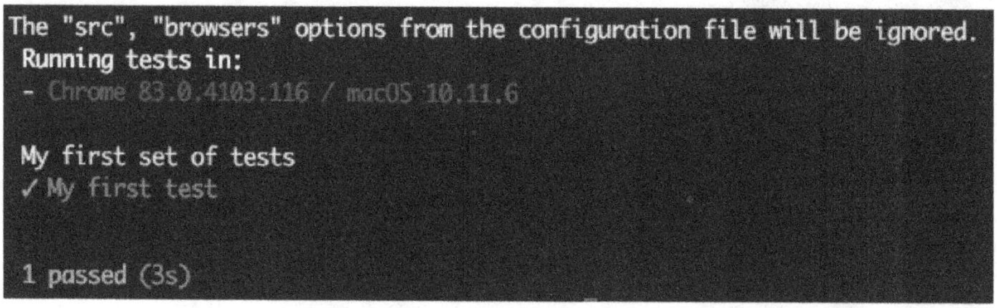

Figure 4.1 – Shell output after the test run

TestCafe will automatically spawn the chosen browser instance and will start running the test. As you can see in the test output: `The "src", "browsers" options from the configuration file will be ignored`. This means that we already specified our default browser and path to the tests in `.testcaferc.json` (you can see it here: `https://github.com/PacktPublishing/Modern-Web-Testing-with-TestCafe/blob/master/ch4/test-project/.testcaferc.json#L3`) and the command shell options that we provided just overrode the defaults.

So, we can now simplify our test run command even more:

```
$ npx testcafe
```

Now TestCafe will just take the default options from `.testcaferc.json` and the result of the test run will be the same. We will review more **Command-Line Interface (CLI)** settings later on in the *Chapter 5, Improving the Tests*.

> **Note**
> Keep the browser that is running tests active and do not minimize the browser window. Minimized browser windows and inactive tabs tend to get shifted to a reduced resource consumption mode where tests are not guaranteed to be executed correctly.

Performing actions

Now let's perform some actions on the page:

```
const { Selector } = require('testcafe');

fixture('My first set of tests')
    .page('http://demo.redmine.org/');

test('My first test', async (t) => {
    await t.click('.login');
});
```

> **Note**
>
> You can also review and download this file on GitHub: `https://github.com/PacktPublishing/Modern-Web-Testing-with-TestCafe/blob/master/ch4/test-project/tests/basic-tests2.js`.

The previous fixture contains a simple test that clicks the **Sign in** link, which we will continue extending further in this chapter. All test actions should be used as async functions of the test controller object t. The test controller object lets us access the API of the test run. The `await` keyword should be used when calling test actions or action chains to wait for them to complete.

As we learned how to run a basic test, let's touch the ground on how to deal with debugging and errors.

Debugging the tests

Now let's see how we can debug our tests. We will review it in two blocks:

- Debugging tests in TestCafe.
- Debugging tests in Chrome Developer Tools.

Let's take a look.

Debugging tests in TestCafe

Let's use the code from the previous example to create a `basic-test-wrong.js` file with a slightly modified class name in the selector:

```
const { Selector } = require('testcafe');

fixture('My first set of tests')
    .page('http://demo.redmine.org/');

test('My first test', async (t) => {
    await t.click('.login-wrong');
});
```

> **Note**
>
> You can also review and download this file on GitHub: `https://github.com/PacktPublishing/Modern-Web-Testing-with-TestCafe/blob/master/ch4/test-project/tests/basic-test-wrong.js`.

The class name `.login-wrong` is used instead of `.login` to provoke the **element not found** error. Let's launch our test to confirm this:

```
$ npx testcafe chrome tests/basic-test-wrong.js
```

The output will look like this:

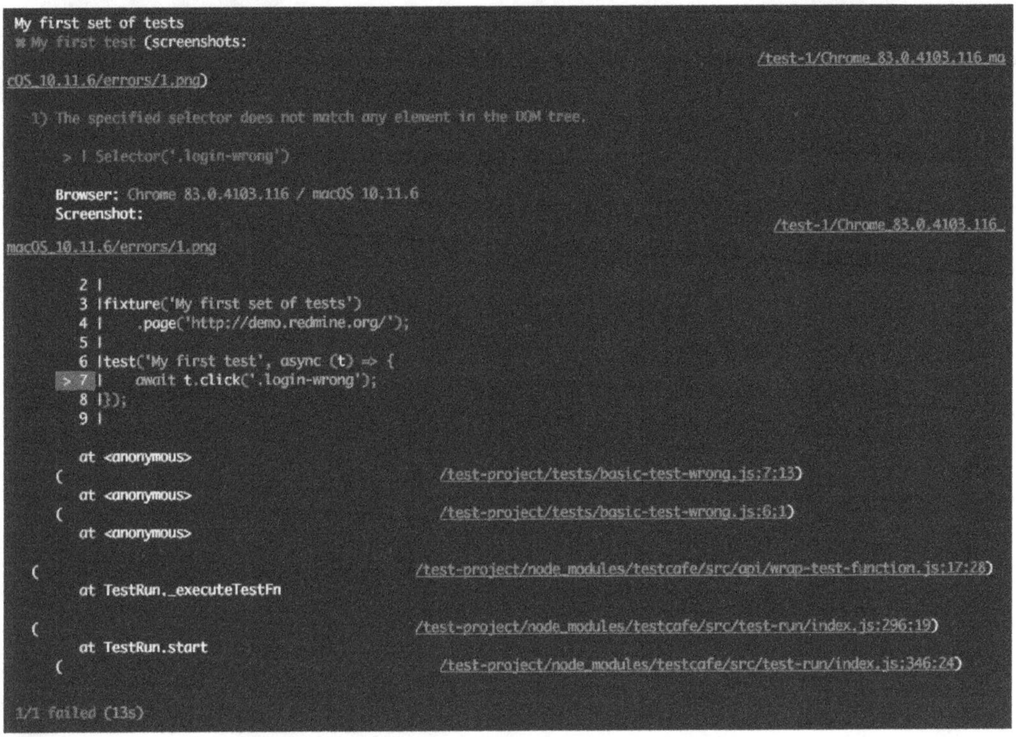

Figure 4.2 – Shell output after the test run with the error

As you can see, TestCafe outputs the error and the line of code where it occurred.

But how do you debug the test even before it failed? For that purpose, TestCafe has the t.debug method. Let's add it to our test:

```
const { Selector } = require('testcafe');

fixture('My first set of tests')
    .page('http://demo.redmine.org/');

test('My first test', async (t) => {
    await t.debug().click('.login-wrong');
});
```

This method is used to pause the test execution and debug it with the browser's developer tools. You will see some buttons to navigate the test run flow in the footer of the browser window:

- **Unlock Page**: Allows us to interact with the browser page that is currently open.

- **Resume**: Allows us to continue the test run.

- **Next Action**: Executes the next action or assertion:

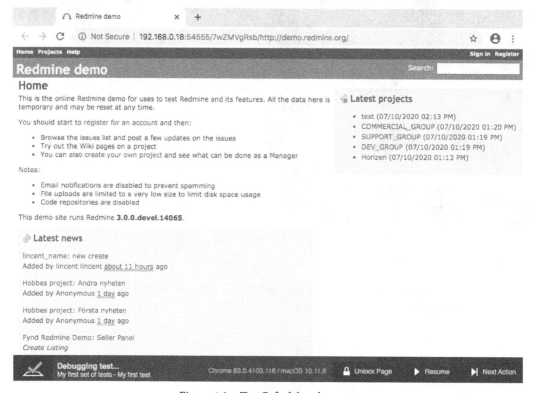

Figure 4.3 – TestCafe debug buttons

And the output will look like this:

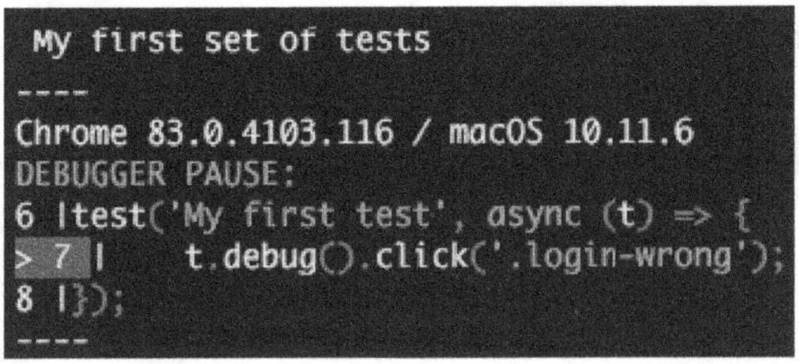

Figure 4.4 – Shell output in debug mode

As you can see, TestCafe outputs the line of code where `t.debug` method is called.

You can also run the tests with `--debug-mode` flag. It will enable debugging and pause the test execution right before the first action or assertion:

```
$ npx testcafe chrome tests/basic-test-wrong.js --debug-mode
```

Or you can use the `--debug-on-fail` flag. It will pause the test when it fails and will allow you to view the tested page and determine the cause of the failure:

```
$ npx testcafe chrome tests/basic-test-wrong.js --debug-on-fail
```

When you are satisfied with the page debugging, just click the **Finish** button in the footer to kill the test execution process.

Now let's see how to debug a test in Chrome Dev Tools.

Debugging tests in Chrome Developer Tools

Another useful way to debug the tests is to do it through Node.js in Chrome Developer Tools. You will need Google Chrome and Node.js v8 or higher to perform all the actions. To debug using the Chrome Developer Tool, follow these steps:

1. Firstly, put the `debugger` keyword in test code where you want the process to stop:

```
const { Selector } = require('testcafe');

fixture('My first set of tests')
    .page('http://demo.redmine.org/');

test('My first test', async (t) => {
    debugger;
    await t.click('.login-wrong');
});
```

2. Then, to activate Node.js debugging mode, add the `--inspect-brk` flag to the test run command:

```
$ npx testcafe --inspect-brk chrome tests/basic-test-
wrong.js
```

3. Open Google Chrome and navigate to `chrome://inspect`. In the **Remote Target** section, find the Node.js debugger and click **Inspect**. Chrome will launch Developer Tools and the debugger will stop test execution at the first line. Click the **Resume script execution** button to continue:

Figure 4.5 – Google Chrome Developer Tools debugger

As you can see the test execution gets paused at the line with `debugger` keyword allowing you to debug the code.

Now, as have learned how to debug the test code, let's go further and write some login tests for our test project.

Writing the test project log in tests

As we discussed in *Chapter 1, Why TestCafe*, we will need a test user to log in to the portal and perform any further tests. So, let's start with creating a new user with an email address – `test_user_testcafe_poc{randomDigits}@sharklasers.com` – and password – `test_user_testcafe_poc`.

Let's declare the following test to register a new user in `basic-tests.js`:

```
const { Selector } = require('testcafe');

fixture('Redmine log in tests')
    .page('http://demo.redmine.org/');

test('Create a new user', async (t) => {
```

The test will perform the following actions:

1. The test clicks on the **Register** link:

   ```
   await t.click('.register')
   ```

2. The test fills in the **Login** field:

   ```
   .typeText('#user_login','test_user_testcafe_
   poc1234@sharklasers.com')
   ```

3. The test fills in the **Password** field:

   ```
   .typeText('#user_password','test_user_testcafe_
   poc')
   ```

4. The test fills in the **Confirmation** field:

   ```
   .typeText('#user_password_confirmation', 'test_
   user_testcafe_poc')
   ```

5. The test fills in the **First name** field:

```
.typeText('#user_firstname','test_user')
```

6. The test fills in the **Last name** field:

```
.typeText('#user_lastname','testcafe_poc')
```

7. The test fills in the **Email** field:

```
.typeText('#user_mail', 'test_user_testcafe_
poc1234@sharklasers.com')
```

8. The test clicks on the **Submit** button:

```
.click('[value="Submit"]');
});
```

> **Note**
>
> You can also review and download this file on GitHub: `https://
> github.com/PacktPublishing/Modern-Web-Testing-
> with-TestCafe/blob/master/ch4/test-project/tests/
> basic-tests3.js`.

As you can see in the previous code block, we are using `1234` as a random number for now. It is simple, but we will have to manually update this number each time we want to create a unique user. Let's improve it to be done automatically by adding a simple open source library that will generate a timestamp for us. Open a shell and execute the following:

```
$ npm install js-automation-tools --save-dev
```

This will install the `js-automation-tools` library and save it to the list of our project's dependencies in `package.json`. Now let's update the code to generate random digits with this library:

```
const { Selector } = require('testcafe');
const { stamp } = require('js-automation-tools');

const randomDigits = stamp.getTimestamp();

fixture('Redmine log in tests')
    .page('http://demo.redmine.org/');
```

```
test('Create a new user', async (t) => {
    await t.click('.register');
        .typeText('#user_login', `test_user_testcafe_
poc${randomDigits}@sharklasers.com`)
        .typeText('#user_password', 'test_user_testcafe_poc')
        .typeText('#user_password_confirmation', 'test_user_
testcafe_poc')
        .typeText('#user_firstname', 'test_user')
        .typeText('#user_lastname', 'testcafe_poc')
        .typeText('#user_mail', `test_user_testcafe_
poc${randomDigits}@sharklasers.com`)
        .click('[value="Submit"]');
});
```

> **Note**
>
> You can also review and download this file on GitHub: `https://github.com/PacktPublishing/Modern-Web-Testing-with-TestCafe/blob/master/ch4/test-project/tests/basic-tests4.js`.

As you can now see, each time we run the test an email with a unique set of digits such as `test_user_testcafe_poc1588556993141@sharklasers.com` is generated, so we don't have to worry about new users anymore.

> **Note**
>
> You can read more about the `js-automation-tools` library and how to use all its features here: `https://github.com/Marketionist/js-automation-tools`.

And so, as we now have a test that creates new Redmine user, let's go forward and add a log in test:

```
const { Selector } = require('testcafe');
const { stamp } = require('js-automation-tools');

const randomDigits = stamp.getTimestamp();

fixture('Redmine log in tests')
    .page('http://demo.redmine.org/');

test('Create a new user', async (t) => {
```

```
    await t.click('.register');
        .typeText('#user_login', `test_user_testcafe_
poc${randomDigits}@sharklasers.com`)
        .typeText('#user_password', 'test_user_testcafe_poc')
        .typeText('#user_password_confirmation', 'test_user_
testcafe_poc')
        .typeText('#user_firstname', 'test_user')
        .typeText('#user_lastname', 'testcafe_poc')
        .typeText('#user_mail', `test_user_testcafe_
poc${randomDigits}@sharklasers.com`)
        .click('[value="Submit"]');
});

test('Log in', async (t) => {
```

The test will perform the following actions:

1. The test clicks on the **Sign in** link:

   ```
   await t.click('.login')
   ```

2. The test fills in the **Login** field:

   ```
       .typeText('#username', `test_user_testcafe_
   poc${randomDigits}@sharklasers.com`)
   ```

3. The test fills in the **Password** field:

   ```
       .typeText('#password', 'test_user_testcafe_poc')
   ```

4. The test clicks on the **Login** button:

   ```
       .click('[name="login"]');
   });
   ```

> **Note**
> You can also review and download this file on GitHub: https://github.
> com/PacktPublishing/Modern-Web-Testing-with-
> TestCafe/blob/master/ch4/test-project/tests/basic-
> tests5.js.

As we now have all actions we need for creating users and logging in, let's add some verifications to make these two tests complete.

Adding verifications to the test project

Normally, each test should perform some actions and then check the result. As we already know from *Chapter 2, Exploring TestCafe Under the hood*, TestCafe provides us with t.expect method to perform the assertions and verify the results of each test. So, let's add corresponding assertions to finalize user creation and log in tests.

Adding assertion for the user creation test

So, the expected result for the user creation test is the **Your account has been activated. You can now log in.** notification, which should be displayed:

```
const { Selector } = require('testcafe');
const { stamp } = require('js-automation-tools');

const randomDigits = stamp.getTimestamp();

fixture('Redmine log in tests')
    .page('http://demo.redmine.org/');

test('Create a new user', async (t) => {
    await t.click('.register');
        .typeText('#user_login', `test_user_testcafe_
poc${randomDigits}@sharklasers.com`)
        .typeText('#user_password', 'test_user_testcafe_poc')
        .typeText('#user_password_confirmation', 'test_user_
testcafe_poc')
        .typeText('#user_firstname', 'test_user')
        .typeText('#user_lastname', 'testcafe_poc')
        .typeText('#user_mail', `test_user_testcafe_
poc${randomDigits}@sharklasers.com`)
        .click('[value="Submit"]')
        .expect(Selector('#flash_notice').innerText).eql('Your
account has been activated. You can now log in.');
});
```

As you can see in the final assertion for the user creation test, we are getting a notification element by its id and then comparing its inner text value with the expected result.

Adding assertion for the log in test

The expected result for the log in test will be a block with the username of the currently active user that should be displayed in the top-right corner of the page:

```
test('Log in', async (t) => {
    await t.click('.login')
        .typeText('#username', `test_user_testcafe_
poc${randomDigits}@sharklasers.com`)
        .typeText('#password', 'test_user_testcafe_poc')
        .click('[name="login"]')
        .expect(Selector('#loggedas').exists).ok();
});
```

> **Note**
>
> You can also review and download this file on GitHub: `https://`
> `github.com/PacktPublishing/Modern-Web-Testing-`
> `with-TestCafe/blob/master/ch4/test-project/tests/`
> `basic-tests6.js`.

To demonstrate one more approach to assertions, in the login test we are verifying that the block with the username of the currently active user is present on the page.

Adding the log out test

Let's also add a log out test to finish up with the `Redmine log in tests` fixture:

```
const { Selector } = require('testcafe');
const { stamp } = require('js-automation-tools');

const randomDigits = stamp.getTimestamp();

fixture('Redmine log in tests')
    .page('http://demo.redmine.org/');

// ...

test('Log out', async (t) => {
    await t.click('.login')
        .typeText('#username', `test_user_testcafe_
poc${randomDigits}@sharklasers.com`)
        .typeText('#password', 'test_user_testcafe_poc')
        .click('[name="login"]')
```

```
        .click('.logout')
        .expect(Selector('#loggedas').exists).notOk()
        .expect(Selector('.login').exists).ok();
});
```

> **Note**
>
> You can also review and download this file on GitHub: `https://github.com/PacktPublishing/Modern-Web-Testing-with-TestCafe/blob/master/ch4/test-project/tests/basic-tests7.js`.

As you can see, we are performing two assertions in the log out test:

1. Verifies that the block with the currently active user is not present on the page.

2. Verifies that the **Sign in** link is present on the page.

As we already have three tests in our test suite, let's add more and review how a custom code can be executed in TestCafe.

Adding custom code execution to the test project

As we already learned from the *Chapter 2, Exploring TestCafe Under the Hood*, TestCafe lets you write code to be executed on the tested page; this way you can get web elements, URLs, and so on. Special kinds of functions are used to execute your code on the client side in the browser:

- `Selector`: To obtain any DOM elements.

- `ClientFunction`: To obtain any data from the client side.

These functions should be used in the same way as ordinary async functions, and you can use parameters to pass data inside such functions. The selector API provides methods and properties to select elements on the page and get their state.

To keep a proper structuring of the tests, it is recommended to group them by fixture. So, let's add a `Redmine entities creation tests` fixture and a `Create a new project` test to see how custom code execution works:

```
const { Selector, ClientFunction } = require('testcafe');
const { stamp } = require('js-automation-tools');

const randomDigits = stamp.getTimestamp();

const getPageUrl = ClientFunction(() => {
    return window.location.href;
});

fixture('Redmine log in tests')
    .page('http://demo.redmine.org/');

// ...

fixture('Redmine entities creation tests')
    .page('http://demo.redmine.org/');

test('Create a new project', async (t) => {
```

The test will perform the following actions:

1. The test logs in:

    ```
        await t.click('.login')
            .typeText('#username', `test_user_testcafe_
    poc${randomDigits}@sharklasers.com`)
            .typeText('#password', 'test_user_testcafe_poc')
            .click('[name="login"]')
    ```

2. The test clicks on the **Projects** link in the top panel:

    ```
            .click('#top-menu .projects')
    ```

3. The test clicks on the **New project** link:

    ```
            .click('.icon-add')
    ```

4. The test fills in the **Name** field:

    ```
            .typeText('#project_name', `test_
    project${randomDigits}`)
    ```

5. The test clicks on the **Create** button:

```
.click('[value="Create"]')
```

6. The test verifies that **Successful creation.** notification is displayed:

```
.expect(Selector('#flash_notice').innerText).
eql('Successful creation.')
```

7. The test verifies that the page URL contains the name of the project:

```
.expect(getPageUrl()).contains(`/projects/test_
project${randomDigits}/settings`);
});
```

> **Note**
>
> You can also review and download this file on GitHub: `https://github.`
> `com/PacktPublishing/Modern-Web-Testing-with-`
> `TestCafe/blob/master/ch4/test-project/tests/basic-`
> `tests8.js`.

As our first fixture contains all login tests, a new fixture was created to include all tests for new entities creation. In addition to that, we added `ClientFunction` and introduced `getPageUrl` function to execute custom code and get the URL of the current page.

And the output will look like this:

```
The "src", "browsers" options from the configuration file will be ignored.
Running tests in:
 - Chrome 83.0.4103.116 / macOS 10.11.6

Redmine log in tests
✓ Create a new user
✓ Log in
✓ Log out

Redmine entities creation tests
✓ Create a new project

4 passed (28s)
```

Figure 4.6 – Shell output with two fixtures

Now, as we have fixtures for Redmine log in tests and Redmine entities creation tests, let's continue filling them up.

Adding more tests

Let's continue writing more tests and structuring them into sets divided by fixtures.

Adding the new issue creation test

We will start from `Create a new issue` test in the `Redmine entities creation tests` fixture:

```
const { Selector, ClientFunction } = require('testcafe');
const { stamp } = require('js-automation-tools');
```

Note how we are creating a second set of random digits. We need them as now the tests are creating two projects, and each project should have a unique name:

```
const randomDigits1 = stamp.getTimestamp();
const randomDigits2 = stamp.resetTimestamp();

const getPageUrl = ClientFunction(() => {
    return window.location.href;
});

fixture('Redmine log in tests')
    .page('http://demo.redmine.org/');

// ...

fixture('Redmine entities creation tests')
    .page('http://demo.redmine.org/');

test('Create a new project', async (t) => {
    await t.click('.login')
        .typeText('#username', `test_user_testcafe_
poc${randomDigits1}@sharklasers.com`)
        .typeText('#password', 'test_user_testcafe_poc')
        .click('[name="login"]')
        .click('#top-menu .projects')
        .click('.icon-add')
        .typeText('#project_name', `test_
project${randomDigits1}`)
        .click('[value="Create"]')
        .expect(Selector('#flash_notice').innerText).
eql('Successful creation.')
        .expect(getPageUrl()).contains(`/projects/test_
project${randomDigits1}/settings`);
```

```
});

test('Create a new issue', async (t) => {
```

The test will perform the following actions:

1. The test logs in:

   ```
   await t.click('.login')
       .typeText('#username', `test_user_testcafe_
   poc${randomDigits1}@sharklasers.com`)
       .typeText('#password', 'test_user_testcafe_poc')
       .click('[name="login"]')
   ```

2. The test creates a new project:

   ```
       .click('#top-menu .projects')
       .click('.icon-add')
       .typeText('#project_name', `test_
   project${randomDigits2}`).click('[value="Create"]')
   ```

3. The test clicks on the **Projects** link in the top panel:

   ```
       .click('#top-menu .projects')
   ```

4. The test clicks on the project link:

   ```
       .click(`[href*="/projects/test_
   project${randomDigits2}"]`)
   ```

5. The test clicks on the **New issue** link:

   ```
       .click('.new-issue')
   ```

6. The test fills in the **Subject** field:

   ```
       .typeText('#issue_subject', `Test issue
   ${randomDigits2}`)
   ```

7. The test fills in the **Description** field:

   ```
       .typeText('#issue_description', `Test issue
   description ${randomDigits2}`)
   ```

8. The test sets **Priority** to **High**:

```
            .click('#issue_priority_id')
            .click('#issue_priority_id option[value="5"]')
```

9. The test clicks on the **Create** button:

```
            .click('[value="Create"]')
```

10. The test verifies that created notification is displayed:

```
            .expect(Selector('#flash_notice').innerText).
    contains('created.');
    });
```

> **Note**
>
> You can also review and download this file on GitHub: https://
> github.com/PacktPublishing/Modern-Web-Testing-
> with-TestCafe/blob/master/ch4/test-project/tests/
> basic-tests9.js.

Adding the new issue is displayed on a project page test

Let's move forward and add a test to verify that the issue is displayed on a project page:

```
const { Selector, ClientFunction } = require('testcafe');
const { stamp } = require('js-automation-tools');

const randomDigits1 = stamp.getTimestamp();
const randomDigits2 = stamp.resetTimestamp();
const randomDigits3 = stamp.resetTimestamp();

// ...

test('Verify that the issue is displayed on a project page',
async (t) => {
```

The test will perform the following actions:

1. The test logs in:

```
await t.click('.login')
    .typeText('#username', `test_user_testcafe_
poc${randomDigits1}@sharklasers.com`)
    .typeText('#password', 'test_user_testcafe_poc')
    .click('[name="login"]')
```

2. The test creates a new project:

```
    .click('#top-menu .projects')
    .click('.icon-add')
    .typeText('#project_name', `test_
project${randomDigits3}`)
    .click('[value="Create"]')
```

3. The test creates a new issue:

```
    .click('#top-menu .projects')
    .click(`[href*="/projects/test_
project${randomDigits3}"]`)
    .click('.new-issue')
    .typeText('#issue_subject', `Test issue
${randomDigits3}`)
    .typeText('#issue_description', `Test issue
description ${randomDigits3}`)
    .click('#issue_priority_id')
    .click('#issue_priority_id option[value="5"]')
    .click('[value="Create"]')
```

4. The test clicks on the **Projects** link in the top panel:

```
    .click('#top-menu .projects')
```

5. The test clicks on the project link:

```
    .click(`[href*="/projects/test_
project${randomDigits3}"]`)
```

6. The test clicks on the **Issues** link:

```
.click('#main-menu .issues')
```

7. The test verifies that the issue's **Subject** is displayed:

```
.expect(Selector('.subject a').innerText).
contains(`Test issue ${randomDigits3}`);
});
```

> **Note**
>
> You can also review and download this file on GitHub: `https://github.com/PacktPublishing/Modern-Web-Testing-with-TestCafe/blob/master/ch4/test-project/tests/basic-tests10.js`.

Adding the issue editing test

Now let's add a new fixture, `Redmine entities editing tests`, and add a test for issue editing:

```
const { Selector, ClientFunction } = require('testcafe');
const { stamp } = require('js-automation-tools');

const randomDigits1 = stamp.getTimestamp();
const randomDigits2 = stamp.resetTimestamp();
const randomDigits3 = stamp.resetTimestamp();
const randomDigits4 = stamp.resetTimestamp();

// ...

fixture('Redmine entities editing tests')
    .page('http://demo.redmine.org/');

test('Edit the issue', async (t) => {
```

The test will perform the following actions:

1. The test logs in:

```
await t.click('.login')
    .typeText('#username', `test_user_testcafe_
poc${randomDigits1}@sharklasers.com`)
```

```
        .typeText('#password', 'test_user_testcafe_poc')
        .click('[name="login"]')
```

2. The test creates a new project:

```
        .click('#top-menu .projects')
        .click('.icon-add')
        .typeText('#project_name', `test_
project${randomDigits4}`)
        .click('[value="Create"]')
```

3. The test creates a new issue:

```
        .click('#top-menu .projects')
        .click(`[href*="/projects/test_
project${randomDigits4}"]`)
        .click('.new-issue')
        .typeText('#issue_subject', `Test issue
${randomDigits4}`)
        .typeText('#issue_description', `Test issue
description ${randomDigits4}`)
        .click('#issue_priority_id')
        .click(Selector('#issue_priority_id option').
withText('High'))
        .click('[value="Create"]')
```

4. The test clicks on the **Projects** link in the top panel:

```
        .click('#top-menu .projects')
```

5. The test clicks on the project link:

```
        .click(`[href*="/projects/test_
project${randomDigits4}"]`)
```

6. The test clicks on the **Issues** link:

```
        .click('#main-menu .issues')
```

7. The test clicks on the issue link:

```
        .click(Selector('.subject a').withText(`Test
issue ${randomDigits4}`))
```

8.   The test clicks on the **Edit** link:

```
.click('.icon-edit')
```

9.   The test clears the **Subject** field and fills it in with a new subject:

```
.selectText('#issue_subject')
.pressKey('delete')
.typeText('#issue_subject', `Issue
${randomDigits4} updated`)
```

10.   The test sets **Priority** to Normal:

```
.click('#issue_priority_id')
.click(Selector('#issue_priority_id option').
withText('Normal'))
```

11.   The test clicks on the **Submit** button:

```
.click('[value="Submit"]')
```

12.   The test verifies that the **Successful update.** notification is displayed:

```
.expect(Selector('#flash_notice').innerText).
eql('Successful update.');
});
```

Note

You can also review and download this file on GitHub: https://github.
com/PacktPublishing/Modern-Web-Testing-with-
TestCafe/blob/master/ch4/test-project/tests/basic-
tests11.js.

There are two interesting things to point out in this code example:

- As CSS selectors cannot access the element's text, the .withText method is used to get the element by its text. Addressing the element by its text is more stable than doing it with option[value="5"] as the value attribute can change if more options will be added to the dropdown. The other possible solution to get the element by its text can be to use XPath selector containing the text.

- The .selectText and .pressKey methods are used to clear the field from its current text. This approach emulates real user behavior. Select all text in the input field and press the *delete* keyboard button to remove it.

Adding the updated issue is displayed on a project page test

Now let's verify that the updated issue is displayed on a project page:

```
const { Selector, ClientFunction } = require('testcafe');
const { stamp } = require('js-automation-tools');

const randomDigits1 = stamp.getTimestamp();
const randomDigits2 = stamp.resetTimestamp();
const randomDigits3 = stamp.resetTimestamp();
const randomDigits4 = stamp.resetTimestamp();
const randomDigits5 = stamp.resetTimestamp();

// ...

test('Verify that the updated issue is displayed on a
project page', async (t) => {
```

The test will perform the following actions:

1. The test logs in:

```
    await t.click('.login')
        .typeText('#username', `test_user_testcafe_
poc${randomDigits1}@sharklasers.com`)
        .typeText('#password', 'test_user_testcafe_poc')
        .click('[name="login"]')
```

2. The test creates a new project:

```
        .click('#top-menu .projects')
        .click('.icon-add')
        .typeText('#project_name', `test_
project${randomDigits5}`)
        .click('[value="Create"]')
```

3. The test creates a new issue:

```
        .click('#top-menu .projects')
        .click(`[href*="/projects/test_
project${randomDigits5}"]`)
        .click('.new-issue')
        .typeText('#issue_subject', `Test issue
${randomDigits5}`)
        .typeText('#issue_description', `Test issue
```

```
        description ${randomDigits5}`)
        .click('#issue_priority_id')
        .click(Selector('#issue_priority_id option').
withText('High'))
        .click('[value="Create"]')
```

4. The test clicks on the **Projects** link in the top panel:

```
        .click('#top-menu .projects')
```

5. The test clicks on the project link:

```
        .click(`[href*="/projects/test_
project${randomDigits5}"]`)
```

6. The test clicks on the **Issues** link:

```
        .click('#main-menu .issues')
```

7. The test clicks on the issue link:

```
        .click(Selector('.subject a').withText(`Test
issue ${randomDigits5}`))
```

8. The test clicks on the **Edit** link:

```
        .click('.icon-edit')
```

9. The test clears the **Subject** field and fills it in with a new subject:

```
        .selectText('#issue_subject')
        .pressKey('delete')
        .typeText('#issue_subject', `Issue
${randomDigits5} updated`)
```

10. The test sets **Priority** to **Normal**:

```
        .click('#issue_priority_id')
        .click(Selector('#issue_priority_id option').
withText('Normal'))
```

11. The test clicks on the **Submit** button:

```
.click('[value="Submit"]')
```

12. The test clicks on the **Issues** link:

```
.click('#main-menu .issues')
```

13. The test verifies that the updated issue's **Subject** is displayed:

```
    .expect(Selector('.subject a').innerText).
eql(`Issue ${randomDigits5} updated`);
});
```

> **Note**
>
> You can also review and download this file on GitHub: https://github.
> com/PacktPublishing/Modern-Web-Testing-with-
> TestCafe/blob/master/ch4/test-project/tests/basic-
> tests12.js.

Adding the issue searching test

Let's add a test for searching the issue:

```
const { Selector, ClientFunction } = require('testcafe');
const { stamp } = require('js-automation-tools');

const randomDigits1 = stamp.getTimestamp();
const randomDigits2 = stamp.resetTimestamp();
const randomDigits3 = stamp.resetTimestamp();
const randomDigits4 = stamp.resetTimestamp();
const randomDigits5 = stamp.resetTimestamp();
const randomDigits6 = stamp.resetTimestamp();

// ...

test('Search for the issue', async (t) => {
```

The test will perform the following actions:

1. The test logs in:

    ```
        await t.click('.login')
            .typeText('#username', `test_user_testcafe_
    poc${randomDigits1}@sharklasers.com`)
                .typeText('#password', 'test_user_testcafe_poc')
                .click('[name="login"]')
    ```

2. The test creates a new project:

    ```
            .click('#top-menu .projects')
            .click('.icon-add')
            .typeText('#project_name', `test_
    project${randomDigits6}`)
            .click('[value="Create"]')
    ```

3. The test creates a new issue:

    ```
            .click('#top-menu .projects')
            .click(`[href*="/projects/test_
    project${randomDigits6}"]`)
            .click('.new-issue')
            .typeText('#issue_subject', `Test issue
    ${randomDigits6}`)
            .typeText('#issue_description', `Test issue
    description ${randomDigits6}`)
            .click('#issue_priority_id')
            .click(Selector('#issue_priority_id option').
    withText('High'))
            .click('[value="Create"]')
    ```

4. The test opens the **Search** page:

    ```
            .navigateTo('http://demo.redmine.org/search')
    ```

5. The test types the issue's subject into the **Search** field:

    ```
            .typeText('#search-input', `Test issue
    ${randomDigits6}`)
    ```

6. The test clicks on the **Submit** button:

```
.click('[value="Submit"]')
```

7. The test verifies that the issue is displayed:

```
.expect(Selector('#search-results').innerText).
contains(`Test issue ${randomDigits6}`);
});
```

> **Note**
> You can also review and download this file on GitHub: `https://github.com/PacktPublishing/Modern-Web-Testing-with-TestCafe/blob/master/ch4/test-project/tests/basic-tests13.js`.

Adding the issue deletion test

Now let's add a `Redmine entities deletion tests` fixture and `Delete the issue` test to demonstrate how to handle native browser dialogs:

```
const { Selector, ClientFunction } = require('testcafe');
const { stamp } = require('js-automation-tools');

const randomDigits1 = stamp.getTimestamp();
const randomDigits2 = stamp.resetTimestamp();
const randomDigits3 = stamp.resetTimestamp();
const randomDigits4 = stamp.resetTimestamp();
const randomDigits5 = stamp.resetTimestamp();
const randomDigits6 = stamp.resetTimestamp();
const randomDigits7 = stamp.resetTimestamp();

// ...

test('Delete the issue', async (t) => {
```

The test will perform the following actions:

1. The test logs in:

```
await t.click('.login')
    .typeText('#username', `test_user_testcafe_
poc${randomDigits1}@sharklasers.com`)
```

```
            .typeText('#password', 'test_user_testcafe_poc')
            .click('[name="login"]')
```

2. The test creates a new project:

```
            .click('#top-menu .projects')
            .click('.icon-add')
            .typeText('#project_name', `test_
    project${randomDigits7}`)
            .click('[value="Create"]')
```

3. The test creates a new issue:

```
            .click('#top-menu .projects')
            .click(`[href*="/projects/test_
    project${randomDigits7}"]`)
            .click('.new-issue')
            .typeText('#issue_subject', `Test issue
    ${randomDigits7}`)
            .typeText('#issue_description', `Test issue
    description ${randomDigits7}`)
            .click('#issue_priority_id')
            .click(Selector('#issue_priority_id option').
    withText('High'))
            .click('[value="Create"]')
```

4. The test clicks on the **Projects** link in the top panel:

```
            .click('#top-menu .projects')
```

5. The test clicks on the project link:

```
            .click(`[href*="/projects/test_
    project${randomDigits7}"]`)
```

6. The test clicks on the **Issues** link:

```
            .click('#main-menu .issues')
```

7. The test clicks on the issue link:

```
            .click(Selector('.subject a').withText(`Test
    issue ${randomDigits7}`))
```

8. The test clicks on the **Delete** link.

9. The test confirms the deletion in the browser modal window:

```
.setNativeDialogHandler(() => true)
.click('.icon-del')
```

10. The test verifies that the issue is not displayed:

```
.expect(Selector('.subject a').withText(`Test
issue ${randomDigits7}`).exists).notOk()
```

11. The test verifies that the **No data to display** notification is displayed:

```
.expect(Selector('.nodata').innerText).eql('No
data to display');
});
```

> **Note**
> You can also review and download this file on GitHub: https://github.com/PacktPublishing/Modern-Web-Testing-with-TestCafe/blob/master/ch4/test-project/tests/basic-tests14.js.

There's one interesting thing to note in this test: we are using the .setNativeDialogHandler method before the browser dialog window will be triggered. We are passing a simple arrow function inside this method: () => true. All it does is just return true. It should be done this way to answer OK (confirm) to the browser dialog window when it will appear (you can read more about this method in *Chapter 2, TestCafe under the Hood*, and here: https://devexpress.github.io/testcafe/documentation/reference/test-api/testcontroller/setnativedialoghandler.html).

Adding the file uploading test

To demonstrate how to work with uploading files, let's add an Upload a file test to the Redmine entities creation tests fixture. But before that, we will need to create a sample file that we will use for uploading, so open a shell and execute the following:

```
$ mkdir -p tests/uploads
$ echo 'test' > uploads/test-file.txt
```

In the preceding commands, we are creating the uploads folder inside the tests folder, and then creating test-file.txt inside it.

Now, as we have a dummy file prepared (you can see it on GitHub too: https://github.com/PacktPublishing/Modern-Web-Testing-with-TestCafe/tree/master/ch4/test-project/tests/uploads/test-file.txt), let's create a file uploading test:

```
const { Selector, ClientFunction } = require('testcafe');
const { stamp } = require('js-automation-tools');

const randomDigits1 = stamp.getTimestamp();
const randomDigits2 = stamp.resetTimestamp();
const randomDigits3 = stamp.resetTimestamp();
const randomDigits4 = stamp.resetTimestamp();
const randomDigits5 = stamp.resetTimestamp();
const randomDigits6 = stamp.resetTimestamp();
const randomDigits7 = stamp.resetTimestamp();
const randomDigits8 = stamp.resetTimestamp();

// ...

test('Upload a file', async (t) => {
```

The test will perform the following actions:

1. The test logs in:

```
await t.click('.login')
    .typeText('#username', `test_user_testcafe_
poc${randomDigits1}@sharklasers.com`)
    .typeText('#password', 'test_user_testcafe_poc')
    .click('[name="login"]')
```

2. The test creates a new project:

```
    .click('#top-menu .projects')
    .click('.icon-add')
    .typeText('#project_name', `test_
project${randomDigits8}`)
    .click('[value="Create"]')
```

3. The test clicks on the **Projects** link in the top panel:

```
.click('#top-menu .projects')
```

4. The test clicks on the project link:

```
.click(`[href*="/projects/test_
project${randomDigits8}"]`)
```

5. The test clicks on the **Files** link:

```
.click('.files')
```

6. The test clicks on the **New file** link:

```
.click('.icon-add')
```

7. The test sets the path to a file:

```
.setFilesToUpload('input.file_selector', './
uploads/test-file.txt')
```

8. The test clicks on the **Add** button:

```
.click('[value="Add"]')
```

9. The test verifies that a link to the file is displayed:

```
.expect(Selector('.filename').innerText).
eql('test-file.txt')
```

10. The test verifies that the MD5 checksum is displayed:

```
.expect(Selector('.digest').innerText).
eql('d8e8fca2dc0f896fd7cb4cb0031ba249');
});
```

> **Note**
>
> You can also review and download this file on GitHub: https://github.
> com/PacktPublishing/Modern-Web-Testing-with-
> TestCafe/blob/master/ch4/test-project/tests/basic-
> tests15.js.

There's one interesting thing to note in this test: we are using the `.setFilesToUpload` method to inject the file path to the file upload input on the page (you can read more about this method in the *Chapter 2, TestCafe under the Hood*, and here: `https://devexpress.github.io/testcafe/documentation/reference/test-api/testcontroller/setfilestoupload.html`).

Adding the file deletion test

Now let's add one final test, `Delete the file`, to the `Redmine entities deletion tests` fixture:

```
const { Selector, ClientFunction } = require('testcafe');
const { stamp } = require('js-automation-tools');

const randomDigits1 = stamp.getTimestamp();
const randomDigits2 = stamp.resetTimestamp();
const randomDigits3 = stamp.resetTimestamp();
const randomDigits4 = stamp.resetTimestamp();
const randomDigits5 = stamp.resetTimestamp();
const randomDigits6 = stamp.resetTimestamp();
const randomDigits7 = stamp.resetTimestamp();
const randomDigits8 = stamp.resetTimestamp();
const randomDigits9 = stamp.resetTimestamp();

// ...

test('Delete the file', async (t) => {
```

The test will perform the following actions:

1. The test logs in:

```
await t.click('.login')
    .typeText('#username', `test_user_testcafe_
poc${randomDigits1}@sharklasers.com`)
    .typeText('#password', 'test_user_testcafe_poc')
    .click('[name="login"]')
```

2. The test creates a new project:

```
.click('#top-menu .projects')
.click('.icon-add')
.typeText('#project_name', `test_
project${randomDigits9}`)
.click('[value="Create"]')
```

3. The test uploads a new file:

```
.click('#top-menu .projects')
.click(`[href*="/projects/test_
project${randomDigits9}"]`)
.click('.files')
.click('.icon-add')
.setFilesToUpload('input.file_selector', './
uploads/test-file.txt')
.click('[value="Add"]')
```

4. The test clicks on the **Projects** link in the top panel:

```
.click('#top-menu .projects')
```

5. The test clicks on the project link:

```
.click(`[href*="/projects/test_
project${randomDigits9}"]`)
```

6. The test clicks on the **Files** link:

```
.click('.files')
```

7. The test clicks on the trash bin icon.

8. The test confirms the deletion in the browser modal window:

```
.setNativeDialogHandler(() => true)
.click(Selector('.filename a').withText('test-
file.txt').parent('.file').find('.buttons a').
withAttribute('data-method', 'delete'))
```

9. The test verifies that a link to the file is not displayed:

    ```
            .expect(Selector('.filename').withText('test-
    file.txt').exists).notOk()
    ```

10. The test verifies that the MD5 checksum is not displayed:

    ```
            .expect(Selector('.digest').
    withText('d8e8fca2dc0f896fd7cb4cb0031ba249').exists).
    notOk();
        });
    ```

> **Note**
>
> You can also review and download this file on GitHub: `https://github.com/PacktPublishing/Modern-Web-Testing-with-TestCafe/blob/master/ch4/test-project/tests/basic-tests16.js`.

One interesting thing to note in this test is how to get the element with a chain of methods: `Selector('.filename a').withText('test-file.txt').parent('.file').find('.buttons a').withAttribute('data-method', 'delete')`. Here, we are getting a link that has `test-file.txt` text, then searching for its parent element with the `file` class, then searching among its descendants for a link with the `data-method="delete"` attribute. This will guarantee that we clicked on the delete link for the corresponding file. You can read more about how to select the elements here: `https://devexpress.github.io/testcafe/documentation/guides/basic-guides/select-page-elements.html`.

Summary

In this chapter, we have concentrated on how to write tests for a real-life project. We crafted four sets of tests (fixtures) for the Redmine demo portal: log in tests, entity creation tests, entity editing tests, and entity deletion tests.

Also, we learned some useful techniques such as how to debug tests, execute custom code, assert elements, clear inputs, press keys, confirm native browser alerts, upload files, and chain element selectors. All of these lessons can be applied to pretty much any other web project.

As our set of tests in now ready, in the next chapter we will be adding setup and teardown sections to our current code to improve its structure and enhance its maintainability.

5
Improving the Tests

The main learning goal of this chapter is to get familiar with how to improve a set of end-to-end tests. This will be achieved with the help of test setup and teardown. Also, we will take a look at different command-line settings to run tests. The testing techniques that we will cover in this chapter are universal and can be reused to write automated tests for any web project. By the end of the chapter, we will have an improved test suite and will learn how to run it with command-line options.

In this chapter, we're going to cover the following main topics:

- Executing selected tests.
- Exploring test setup and teardown.
- Adding setup and teardown to the test project.
- Running tests with command-line settings.

Technical requirements

All of the code examples for this chapter can be found on GitHub at `https://github.com/PacktPublishing/Modern-Web-Testing-with-TestCafe/blob/master/ch5`.

Executing selected tests

Quite often, when writing or extending a set of tests, we need to concentrate on one specific test while omitting all others. Tests are usually organized into sets (groups of tests are also known as fixtures). Luckily, TestCafe provides the `fixture.only` and `test.only` methods to specify that only a selected test or fixture should be executed and all others should be skipped. Let's review it using our set of tests in a simplified form, with all the test actions commented out:

```
// ...

fixture('Redmine log in tests')
    .page('http://demo.redmine.org/');

test.only('Create a new user', async (t) => { /* ... */ });

test('Log in', async (t) => { /* ... */ });

test('Log out', async (t) => { /* ... */ });

fixture('Redmine entities creation tests')
    .page('http://demo.redmine.org/');

test('Create a new project', async (t) => { /* ... */ });

test('Create a new issue', async (t) => { /* ... */ });

test('Verify that the issue is displayed on a project page',
async (t) => { /* ... */ });

test('Upload a file', async (t) => { /* ... */ });

fixture('Redmine entities editing tests')
    .page('http://demo.redmine.org/');

test('Edit the issue', async (t) => { /* ... */ });

test('Verify that the updated issue is displayed on a project
page', async (t) => { /* ... */ });

test('Search for the issue', async (t) => { /* ... */ });

fixture.only('Redmine entities deletion tests')
    .page('http://demo.redmine.org/');
```

```
test('Delete the issue', async (t) => { /* ... */ });

test('Delete the file', async (t) => { /* ... */ });
```

As you can see in the example, `test.only` is used in the `Create a new user` test, and `fixture.only` is used in the `Redmine entities deletion tests` fixture, so only the `Create a new user`, `Delete the issue`, and `Delete the file` tests will be executed.

> **Note**
>
> If several tests (or fixtures) are marked with `test.only` (or `fixture.only`), all the marked tests and fixtures will be executed.

In addition to that, TestCafe allows you to use the `test.skip` and `fixture.skip` methods to specify a test or a fixture to skip when tests run:

```
// ...

fixture('Redmine log in tests')
    .page('http://demo.redmine.org/');

test('Create a new user', async (t) => { /* ... */ });

test.skip('Log in', async (t) => { /* ... */ });

test.skip('Log out', async (t) => { /* ... */ });

fixture.skip('Redmine entities creation tests')
    .page('http://demo.redmine.org/');

test('Create a new project', async (t) => { /* ... */ });

test('Create a new issue', async (t) => { /* ... */ });

test('Verify that the issue is displayed on a project page',
async (t) => { /* ... */ });

test('Upload a file', async (t) => { /* ... */ });

fixture('Redmine entities editing tests')
    .page('http://demo.redmine.org/');

test('Edit the issue', async (t) => { /* ... */ });
```

```
test.skip('Verify that the updated issue is displayed on a
project page', async (t) => { /* ... */ });

test.skip('Search for the issue', async (t) => { /* ... */ });

fixture.skip('Redmine entities deletion tests')
    .page('http://demo.redmine.org/');

test('Delete the issue', async (t) => { /* ... */ });

test('Delete the file', async (t) => { /* ... */ });
```

As demonstrated in the preceding example, only the `Create a new user` and `Edit the issue` tests will be executed.

Now that we have learned how to execute a particular test or fixture, skipping all the others, let's see how test setup and teardown can be done.

Exploring test setup and teardown

As tests can be quite long and contain a lot of repetitive actions, TestCafe has a way to optimize this with test setup and teardown.

Setup is usually done by executing a number of specific functions (also known as hooks) *before* a fixture or test starts (including `fixture.before`, `fixture.beforeEach`, and `test.before`).

Teardown is usually done by executing a number of specific functions *after* a fixture or test is completed (including `fixture.after`, `fixture.afterEach`, and `test.after`).

There are six methods for using hooks in TestCafe.

The first two (`fixture.before` and `fixture.after`) do not have access to the tested page and thus should be used to perform server-side operations, such as preparing the tested application's server or pre-creating some test data in the database:

- `fixture.before` can be used to specify actions that should be executed before the first test in a fixture starts (`https://devexpress.github.io/testcafe/documentation/reference/test-api/fixture/before.html`). In the following example, the `createTestData` function will be called before the first test of the `My first set of tests` fixture:

    ```
    fixture('My first set of tests')
        .page('https://test-site.com')
    ```

```
    .before(async (t) => {
        await createTestData();
    });
```

- `fixture.after` can be used to specify actions that should be executed after the last test in a fixture is finished (`https://devexpress.github.io/testcafe/documentation/reference/test-api/fixture/after.html`). In the following example, the `deleteTestData` function will be called after the last test of the `My first set of tests` fixture:

```
fixture('My first set of tests')
    .page('https://test-site.com')
    .after(async (t) => {
        await deleteTestData();
    });
```

The next four methods (`fixture.beforeEach`, `fixture.afterEach`, `test.before`, and `test.after`) are launched when the tested web page is already loaded, so you can execute test actions and other test API methods inside these test hooks:

- `fixture.beforeEach` can be used to specify actions that should be executed before each test in a fixture (`https://devexpress.github.io/testcafe/documentation/reference/test-api/fixture/beforeeach.html`). In the following example, the `click` action will be performed before each test of the `My first set of tests` fixture:

```
fixture('My first set of tests')
    .page('https://test-site.com')
    .beforeEach(async (t) => {
        await t.click('#log-in');
    });
```

- `fixture.afterEach` can be used to specify actions that should be executed after each test in a fixture (`https://devexpress.github.io/testcafe/documentation/reference/test-api/fixture/aftereach.html`). In the following example, the `click` action will be performed after each test of the `My first set of tests` fixture:

```
fixture('My first set of tests')
    .page('https://test-site.com')
    .afterEach(async (t) => {
        await t.click('#delete-test-data');
    });
```

- `test.before` can be used to specify actions that should be executed before a particular test (`https://devexpress.github.io/testcafe/documentation/reference/test-api/test/before.html`). In the following example, the `click` action will be performed before the `My first Test` test:

```
test
    .before(async (t) => {
        await t.click('#log-in');
    })
    ('My first Test', async (t) => { /* ... */ });
```

- `test.after` can be used to specify actions that should be executed after a particular test (`https://devexpress.github.io/testcafe/documentation/reference/test-api/test/after.html`). In the following example, the `click` action will be performed after the `My first Test` test:

```
test
    .after(async (t) => {
        await t.click('#delete-test-data');
    })
    ('My first Test', async (t) => { /* ... */ });
```

> **Note**
>
> If a test runs in several browsers, test hooks are executed in each browser. If both the `fixture.beforeEach` and `test.before` (or `fixture.afterEach` and `test.after`) hooks are used together, the most specific hook will overrule. So, `test.before` (or `test.after`) will be executed and `fixture.beforeEach` (or `fixture.afterEach`) will be omitted and will not run for this test.

You can read more about the hooks at `https://devexpress.github.io/testcafe/documentation/guides/basic-guides/organize-tests.html#initialization-and-clean-up`.

In this section, we went through the types of hooks that are available in TestCafe. Now, let's put this knowledge into practice by applying it to our set of tests.

Adding setup and teardown to the test project

In this section, we will see how to optimize our test project code with setup and teardown blocks.

As we saw in the *Exploring test setup and teardown* section, `fixture.beforeEach` can specifically be useful when each of the tests needs a user to be logged in before the test. That's exactly our case, so let's add the `beforeEach` block to the `Redmine entities creation tests` fixture:

```
// ...

fixture('Redmine entities creation tests')
    .page('http://demo.redmine.org/')
    .beforeEach(async (t) => {
        await t.click('.login')
            .typeText('#username', `test_user_testcafe_
poc${randomDigits1}@sharklasers.com`)
            .typeText('#password', 'test_user_testcafe_poc')
            .click('[name="login"]');
    });
```

Let's also remove the login actions from all the tests of the `Redmine entities creation tests` fixture, as these actions will be executed in the `beforeEach` block. So, the `Create a new project` test will look like this:

```
test('Create a new project', async (t) => {
    await t.click('#top-menu .projects')
        .click('.icon-add')
        .typeText('#project_name', `test_
project${randomDigits1}`)
        .click('[value="Create"]')
        .expect(Selector('#flash_notice').innerText).
eql('Successful creation.')
        .expect(getPageUrl()).contains(`/projects/test_
project${randomDigits1}/settings`);
});
```

After all login actions were moved to the `beforeEach` block, the `Create a new issue` test will look like this:

```
test('Create a new issue', async (t) => {
    await t.click('#top-menu .projects')
        .click('.icon-add')
        .typeText('#project_name', `test_
project${randomDigits2}`)
        .click('[value="Create"]')
```

```
        .click('#top-menu .projects')
        .click(`[href*="/projects/test_
project${randomDigits2}"]`)
        .click('.new-issue')
        .typeText('#issue_subject', `Test issue
${randomDigits2}`)
        .typeText('#issue_description', `Test issue description
${randomDigits2}`)
        .click('#issue_priority_id')
        .click(Selector('#issue_priority_id option').
withText('High'))
        .click('[value="Create"]')
        .expect(Selector('#flash_notice').innerText).
contains('created.');
});
```

And the `Verify that the issue is displayed on a project page` test, without login actions, will look like this:

```
test('Verify that the issue is displayed on a project page',
async (t) => {
    await t.click('#top-menu .projects')
        .click('.icon-add')
        .typeText('#project_name', `test_
project${randomDigits3}`)
        .click('[value="Create"]')
        .click('#top-menu .projects')
        .click(`[href*="/projects/test_
project${randomDigits3}"]`)
        .click('.new-issue')
        .typeText('#issue_subject', `Test issue
${randomDigits3}`)
        .typeText('#issue_description', `Test issue description
${randomDigits3}`)
        .click('#issue_priority_id')
        .click(Selector('#issue_priority_id option').
withText('High'))
        .click('[value="Create"]')
        .click('#top-menu .projects')
        .click(`[href*="/projects/test_
project${randomDigits3}"]`)
        .click('#main-menu .issues')
        .expect(Selector('.subject a').innerText).
```

```
contains(`Test issue ${randomDigits3}`);
});
```

And finally, the `Upload a file` test without login actions will look like this:

```
test('Upload a file', async (t) => {
    await t.click('#top-menu .projects')
        .click('.icon-add')
        .typeText('#project_name', `test_
project${randomDigits8}`)
        .click('[value="Create"]')
        .click('#top-menu .projects')
        .click(`[href*="/projects/test_
project${randomDigits8}"]`)
        .click('.files')
        .click('.icon-add')
        .setFilesToUpload('input.file_selector', './uploads/
test-file.txt')
        .click('[value="Add"]')
        .expect(Selector('.filename').innerText).eql('test-
file.txt')
        .expect(Selector('.digest').innerText).
eql('d8e8fca2dc0f896fd7cb4cb0031ba249');
});
```

Now, let's add the `beforeEach` block to the `Redmine entities editing tests` fixture:

```
fixture('Redmine entities editing tests')
    .page('http://demo.redmine.org/')
    .beforeEach(async (t) => {
        await t.click('.login')
            .typeText('#username', `test_user_testcafe_
poc${randomDigits1}@sharklasers.com`)
            .typeText('#password', 'test_user_testcafe_poc')
            .click('[name="login"]');
    });
```

Let's also remove the login actions from all the tests of the `Redmine entities editing tests` fixture, as this action will now be executed in the `beforeEach` block. So, the `Edit the issue` test will look like this:

```
test('Edit the issue', async (t) => {
    await t.click('#top-menu .projects')
        .click('.icon-add')
        .typeText('#project_name', `test_
project${randomDigits4}`)
        .click('[value="Create"]')
        .click('#top-menu .projects')
        .click(`[href*="/projects/test_
project${randomDigits4}"]`)
        .click('.new-issue')
        .typeText('#issue_subject', `Test issue
${randomDigits4}`)
        .typeText('#issue_description', `Test issue description
${randomDigits4}`)
        .click('#issue_priority_id')
        .click(Selector('#issue_priority_id option').
withText('High'))
        .click('[value="Create"]')
        .click('#top-menu .projects')
        .click(`[href*="/projects/test_
project${randomDigits4}"]`)
        .click('#main-menu .issues')
        .click(Selector('.subject a').withText(`Test issue
${randomDigits4}`))
        .click('.icon-edit')
        .selectText('#issue_subject')
        .pressKey('delete')
        .typeText('#issue_subject', `Issue ${randomDigits4}
updated`)
        .click('#issue_priority_id')
        .click(Selector('#issue_priority_id option').
withText('Normal'))
        .click('[value="Submit"]')
        .expect(Selector('#flash_notice').innerText).
eql('Successful update.');
});
```

All login actions were moved to the beforeEach block, so the Verify that the updated issue is displayed on a project page test will look like this:

```
test('Verify that the updated issue is displayed on a project
page', async (t) => {
    await t.click('#top-menu .projects')
        .click('.icon-add')
```

```
        .typeText('#project_name', `test_
project${randomDigits5}`)
        .click('[value="Create"]')
        .click('#top-menu .projects')
        .click(`[href*="/projects/test_
project${randomDigits5}"]`)
        .click('.new-issue')
        .typeText('#issue_subject', `Test issue
${randomDigits5}`)
        .typeText('#issue_description', `Test issue description
${randomDigits5}`)
        .click('#issue_priority_id')
        .click(Selector('#issue_priority_id option').
withText('High'))
        .click('[value="Create"]')
        .click('#top-menu .projects')
        .click(`[href*="/projects/test_
project${randomDigits5}"]`)
        .click('#main-menu .issues')
        .click(Selector('.subject a').withText(`Test issue
${randomDigits5}`))
        .click('.icon-edit')
        .selectText('#issue_subject')
        .pressKey('delete')
        .typeText('#issue_subject', `Issue ${randomDigits5}
updated`)
        .click('#issue_priority_id')
        .click(Selector('#issue_priority_id option').
withText('Normal'))
        .click('[value="Submit"]')
        .click('#main-menu .issues')
        .expect(Selector('.subject a').innerText).eql(`Issue
${randomDigits5} updated`);
});
```

The `Search for the issue` test without all login actions will look like this:

```
test('Search for the issue', async (t) => {
    await t.click('#top-menu .projects')
        .click('.icon-add')
        .typeText('#project_name', `test_
project${randomDigits6}`)
        .click('[value="Create"]')
        .click('#top-menu .projects')
```

```
        .click(`[href*="/projects/test_
project${randomDigits6}"]`)
        .click('.new-issue')
        .typeText('#issue_subject', `Test issue
${randomDigits6}`)
        .typeText('#issue_description', `Test issue description
${randomDigits6}`)
        .click('#issue_priority_id')
        .click(Selector('#issue_priority_id option').
withText('High'))
        .click('[value="Create"]')
        .navigateTo('http://demo.redmine.org/search')
        .typeText('#search-input', `Test issue
${randomDigits6}`)
        .click('[value="Submit"]')
        .expect(Selector('#search-results').innerText).
contains(`Test issue ${randomDigits6}`);
});
```

Now, let's add the `beforeEach` block to the `Redmine entities deletion tests` fixture:

```
fixture('Redmine entities deletion tests')
    .page('http://demo.redmine.org/')
    .beforeEach(async (t) => {
        await t.click('.login')
            .typeText('#username', `test_user_testcafe_
poc${randomDigits1}@sharklasers.com`)
            .typeText('#password', 'test_user_testcafe_poc')
            .click('[name="login"]');
});
```

Let's also remove the login actions from all the tests of the `Redmine entities deletion tests` fixture, as these actions will now be executed in the `beforeEach` block. So, the `Delete the issue` test will look like this:

```
test('Delete the issue', async (t) => {
    await t.click('#top-menu .projects')
        .click('.icon-add')
        .typeText('#project_name', `test_
project${randomDigits7}`)
        .click('[value="Create"]')
        .click('#top-menu .projects')
```

```
        .click(`[href*="/projects/test_
project${randomDigits7}"]`)
        .click('.new-issue')
        .typeText('#issue_subject', `Test issue
${randomDigits7}`)
        .typeText('#issue_description', `Test issue description
${randomDigits7}`)
        .click('#issue_priority_id')
        .click(Selector('#issue_priority_id option').
withText('High'))
        .click('[value="Create"]')
        .click('#top-menu .projects')
        .click(`[href*="/projects/test_
project${randomDigits7}"]`)
        .click('#main-menu .issues')
        .click(Selector('.subject a').withText(`Test issue
${randomDigits7}`))
        .setNativeDialogHandler(() => true)
        .click('.icon-del')
        .expect(Selector('.subject a').withText(`Test issue
${randomDigits7}`).exists).notOk()
        .expect(Selector('.nodata').innerText).eql('No data to
display');
});
```

And the `Delete the file` test, after all login actions were moved to the `beforeEach` block, will look like this:

```
test('Delete the file', async (t) => {
    await t.click('#top-menu .projects')
        .click('.icon-add')
        .typeText('#project_name', `test_
project${randomDigits9}`)
        .click('[value="Create"]')
        .click('#top-menu .projects')
        .click(`[href*="/projects/test_
project${randomDigits9}"]`)
        .click('.files')
        .click('.icon-add')
        .setFilesToUpload('input.file_selector', './uploads/
test-file.txt')
        .click('[value="Add"]')
        .click('#top-menu .projects')
        .click(`[href*="/projects/test_
```

```
                 project${randomDigits9}"]`)
          .click('.files')
          .setNativeDialogHandler(() => true)
          .click(Selector('.filename a').withText('test-file.
txt').parent('.file').find('.buttons a').withAttribute('data-
method', 'delete'))
          .expect(Selector('.filename').withText('test-file.
txt').exists).notOk()
          .expect(Selector('.digest').
withText('d8e8fca2dc0f896fd7cb4cb0031ba249').exists).
notOk();
});
```

> **Note**
>
> You can also review and download this file on GitHub at `https://github.com/PacktPublishing/Modern-Web-Testing-with-TestCafe/blob/master/ch5/test-project/tests/basic-tests17.js`.

As we have integrated setup and teardown blocks, let's see how to run tests with command-line settings.

Running tests with command-line settings

As we already learned in *Chapter 3, Setting Up the Environment*, when you trigger tests by executing the `testcafe` command, TestCafe reads settings from the `.testcaferc.json` configuration file, if this file exists, and then applies the settings from the command line on top of it. Command-line settings overrule values from the configuration file if they differ. TestCafe outputs information about each overridden property to the console.

> **Note**
>
> If the `browsers` and `src` properties are provided in the configuration file, you can omit them in the command line.

Let's review some of the main command-line settings that can be used with the `testcafe` command while launching the tests:

- `--help`, or `-h`, outputs a list of all the available command-line options (https://devexpress.github.io/testcafe/documentation/reference/command-line-interface.html#-h---help). Open any shell and run the following:

    ```
    $ npx testcafe --help
    ```

- `--quarantine-mode`, or `-q`, enables quarantine mode for tests that fail (https://devexpress.github.io/testcafe/documentation/reference/command-line-interface.html#-q---quarantine-mode). Open any shell and run the following:

    ```
    $ npx testcafe chrome tests/basic-tests.js --quarantine-mode
    ```

- `--debug-mode`, or `-d`, executes test steps one by one, pausing the test after each step for debugging (https://devexpress.github.io/testcafe/documentation/reference/command-line-interface.html#-d---debug-mode). Open any shell and run the following:

    ```
    $ npx testcafe chrome tests/basic-tests.js --debug-mode
    ```

- `--debug-on-fail`: If a test fails, automatically pause it and enter debug mode (https://devexpress.github.io/testcafe/documentation/reference/command-line-interface.html#--debug-on-fail). Open any shell and run the following:

    ```
    $ npx testcafe chrome tests/basic-tests.js --debug-on-fail
    ```

- `--disable-page-caching` disables browser page caching during test execution (https://devexpress.github.io/testcafe/documentation/reference/command-line-interface.html#--disable-page-caching). Open any shell and run the following:

    ```
    $ npx testcafe chrome tests/basic-tests.js --disable-page-caching
    ```

- `--skip-js-errors`, or `-e`, makes sure tests don't fail when a JavaScript error occurs on a tested page (`https://devexpress.github.io/testcafe/documentation/reference/command-line-interface.html#-e---skip-js-errors`). Open any shell and run the following:

```
$ npx testcafe chrome tests/basic-tests.js --skip-js-
errors
```

- `--skip-uncaught-errors`, or `-u`, ignores uncaught errors and unhandled promise rejections that occur during test execution (`https://devexpress.github.io/testcafe/documentation/reference/command-line-interface.html#-u---skip-uncaught-errors`). Open any shell and run the following:

```
$ npx testcafe chrome tests/basic-tests.js --skip-
uncaught-errors
```

- `--test <name>`, or `-t <name>`, only runs tests with the specified name (`https://devexpress.github.io/testcafe/documentation/reference/command-line-interface.html#-t-name---test-name`). Open any shell and run the following:

```
$ npx testcafe chrome tests/basic-tests.js --test "Click
a link"
```

- `--test-grep <pattern>`, or `-T <pattern>`, only runs tests matching the specified pattern (`https://devexpress.github.io/testcafe/documentation/reference/command-line-interface.html#-t-pattern---test-grep-pattern`). For example, to run tests whose names are `Click a link`, `Click a dropdown`, and so on, open any shell and run the following:

```
$ npx testcafe chrome tests/basic-tests.js --test-grep
"Click.*"
```

- `--fixture <name>`, or `-f <name>`, only runs tests from the fixtures with the specified name (`https://devexpress.github.io/testcafe/documentation/reference/command-line-interface.html#-f-name---fixture-name`). Open any shell and run the following:

```
$ npx testcafe chrome tests/basic-tests.js --fixture "My
first Fixture"
```

- `--fixture-grep <pattern>`, or `-F <pattern>`, only runs tests from the fixtures matching the specified pattern (`https://devexpress.github.io/testcafe/documentation/reference/command-line-interface.html#-f-pattern---fixture-grep-pattern`). For example, to run tests from the fixtures whose names are `Suite1`, `Suite2`, and so on, open any shell and run the following:

```
$ npx testcafe chrome tests/basic-tests.js --fixture-grep
"Suite.*"
```

- `--test-meta <key=value[,key2=value2,...]>` runs tests whose metadata matches the specified key-value pair (`https://devexpress.github.io/testcafe/documentation/reference/command-line-interface.html#--test-meta-keyvaluekey2value2`). For example, to run tests whose metadata's `suite` property is set to `fast` and `env` property is set to `staging`, open any shell and run the following:

```
$ npx testcafe chrome tests/basic-tests.js --test-meta
suite=fast,env=staging
```

- `--fixture-meta <key=value[,key2=value2,...]>` runs tests from fixtures whose metadata matches the specified key-value pair (`https://devexpress.github.io/testcafe/documentation/reference/command-line-interface.html#--fixture-meta-keyvaluekey2value2`). For example, to run tests from fixtures whose metadata's `suite` property is set to `long` and `env` property is set to `production`, open any shell and run the following:

```
$ npx testcafe chrome tests/basic-tests.js --fixture-meta
suite=long,env=production
```

- `--app <command>`, or `-a <command>`, executes the specified shell command before tests are started, and is often used to launch the tested app using the specified command before running tests (`https://devexpress.github.io/testcafe/documentation/reference/command-line-interface.html#-a-command---app-command`). Open any shell and run the following:

```
$ npx testcafe chrome tests/basic-tests.js --app "node
index.js"
```

- `--concurrency <number>`, or `-c <number>`, runs tests in parallel (concurrently) by spawning the provided number of browser instances (`https://devexpress.github.io/testcafe/documentation/reference/command-line-interface.html#-c-n---concurrency-n`). Open any shell and run the following:

  ```
  $ npx testcafe chrome tests/basic-tests.js --concurrency 4
  ```

- `--speed <factor>` sets the speed of test execution from the slowest, `0.01`, to the fastest, `1` (`https://devexpress.github.io/testcafe/documentation/reference/command-line-interface.html#--speed-factor`). Open any shell and run the following:

  ```
  $ npx testcafe chrome tests/basic-tests.js --speed 0.8
  ```

You can read more about all the command-line options at `https://devexpress.github.io/testcafe/documentation/reference/command-line-interface.html`.

It is good practice to keep all the major settings in the `.testcaferc.json` configuration file, overriding them with command-line settings when needed – for example, a combination of `--debug-on-fail --speed 0.8` will be quite convenient for debugging.

To sum up, in this section we learned about some of the main command-line settings and how they can be used when launching tests.

Summary

In this chapter, we explored how to execute tests selectively, as well as how to generalize some test actions with the help of test setup and teardown. Also, we reviewed some command-line settings to run tests. Now we have an improved test suite and know how to run it with command-line options.

In the next chapter, we will continue to refine our test suite by moving some test logic to separate functions and refactoring tests with `PageObjects`.

6
Refactoring with PageObjects

The main learning goal here will be to get familiar with how to upgrade a set of end-to-end tests (test suite) with a TestCafe role and the `PageObject` pattern. We will use `Role` to speed up the tests and will utilize `PageObjects` to achieve reduced code duplication and enhanced maintainability. By the end of this chapter, we will have a structured and optimized set of tests and know how to apply roles and `PageObject` patterns to any future projects.

In this chapter, we're going to cover the following main topics:

- Adding a `Role` for logging in.
- Refactoring tests with `PageObjects`.
- Improving `PageObjects` with functions.

Technical requirements

All the code examples for this chapter can be found on GitHub: `https://github.com/PacktPublishing/Modern-Web-Testing-with-TestCafe/tree/master/ch6`.

Adding a Role for logging in

As we already learned from *Chapter 2*, *Exploring TestCafe under the Hood*, TestCafe has a built-in user role mechanism that emulates user actions for logging in to a website. The role mechanism saves the logged-in state of each user in a separate role that can then be reused in any part of your tests to switch between user accounts.

So, let's start by adding a `Role` to optimize and speed up the logging-in process that we perform in each test:

```
const { Selector, ClientFunction, Role } = require('testcafe');

// ...

const regularUser = Role('http://demo.redmine.org/', async (t)
=> {
    await t.click('.login')
        .typeText('#username', `test_user_testcafe_
poc${randomDigits1}@sharklasers.com`)
        .typeText('#password', 'test_user_testcafe_poc')
        .click('[name="login"]');
});
```

As you can see, we are using the login steps inside the `Role`. These steps will be executed when the `regularUser` role is called for the first time. Once the login steps are executed, the final (logged-in) state of the authentication cookie and browser storage will be saved and reused in each further call of the `regularUser` role (login steps will not be executed again, as a saved logged-in state will be applied). Now, let's use the `regularUser` role in the `Log out` test:

```
test('Log out', async (t) => {
    await t.useRole(regularUser)
        .click('.logout')
        .expect(Selector('#loggedas').exists).notOk()
        .expect(Selector('.login').exists).ok();
});
```

Let's also replace the login steps with the `regularUser` role in the `beforeEach` blocks of all other fixtures:

```
// ...

fixture('Redmine entities creation tests')
    .page('http://demo.redmine.org/')
    .beforeEach(async (t) => {
```

```
        await t.useRole(regularUser);
    });

// ...

fixture('Redmine entities editing tests')
    .page('http://demo.redmine.org/')
    .beforeEach(async (t) => {
        await t.useRole(regularUser);
    });

// ...

fixture('Redmine entities deletion tests')
    .page('http://demo.redmine.org/')
    .beforeEach(async (t) => {
        await t.useRole(regularUser);
    });

// ...
```

Note

You can also review and download this file on GitHub: `https://github.com/PacktPublishing/Modern-Web-Testing-with-TestCafe/blob/master/ch6/test-project/tests/basic-tests18.js`.

Utilizing roles speeds up execution of the test and our test project becomes more structured and granular, which is a good approach to follow.

As we have built our set of tests, improved them with setup, teardown, and roles, let's now make them even more effective and maintainable by refactoring with `PageObjects`.

Refactoring tests with PageObjects

`PageObject` is a test automation pattern that gives you the option to create a separate file with selectors and functions that represent an abstraction of the tested page. This separate file can then be included and used in test code to refer to page elements.

Note that our tests contain excessive code. For example, the #top-menu .projects CSS selector (https://github.com/PacktPublishing/Modern-Web-Testing-with-TestCafe/blob/master/ch6/test-project/tests/basic-tests18.js#L62) is used in 22 lines of code - basically each time the test clicks on the **Projects** link. In the modern world of fast-paced web development, page design and mark-ups may evolve and change quite often. Each time this happens, selectors in all corresponding tests will need to be modified. PageObjects allow you to keep all selectors in one place, so the next time the web page changes, you will only need to modify the PageObject file.

So, let's create a simple redmine-page.js file inside our tests folder. Open any shell, go to the test-project folder, and execute the following command:

```
$ touch tests/redmine-page.js
```

Now, open the redmine-page.js file in a code editor of your choice, add the code to declare the linkProjects selector inside the redminePage object, and then export this object:

```
let redminePage = {
    linkProjects: '#top-menu .projects'
};

module.exports = redminePage;
```

> **Note**
>
> You can also review and download this file on GitHub: https://github.com/PacktPublishing/Modern-Web-Testing-with-TestCafe/blob/master/ch6/test-project/tests/redmine-page1.js.

So, we created a redminePage object with a linkProjects property containing a selector for this element. Now we need to include this object in our tests:

```
const { Selector, ClientFunction, Role } = require('testcafe');
const { stamp } = require('js-automation-tools');

const redminePage = require('./redmine-page.js');

// ...
```

In addition to that, we will need to replace all occurrences of #top-menu .projects with a corresponding PageObject element. So, here is how the updated Create a new project test will appear:

```
test('Create a new project', async (t) => {
    await t.click(redminePage.linkProjects)
        .click('.icon-add')
        .typeText('#project_name', `test_
project${randomDigits1}`)
        .click('[value="Create"]')
        .expect(Selector('#flash_notice').innerText).
eql('Successful creation.')
        .expect(getPageUrl()).contains(`/projects/test_
project${randomDigits1}/settings`);
});
```

> **Note**
>
> You can also review and download this file with all the tests updated to use redminePage.linkProjects on GitHub: https://github.com/PacktPublishing/Modern-Web-Testing-with-TestCafe/blob/master/ch6/test-project/tests/basic-tests19.js.

Let's now move all constants with random digit generation to redmine-page.js, as all the strings that are using random digits will be moved to redmine-page.js too:

```
const { stamp } = require('js-automation-tools');

const randomDigits1 = stamp.getTimestamp();
const randomDigits2 = stamp.resetTimestamp();
const randomDigits3 = stamp.resetTimestamp();
const randomDigits4 = stamp.resetTimestamp();
const randomDigits5 = stamp.resetTimestamp();
const randomDigits6 = stamp.resetTimestamp();
const randomDigits7 = stamp.resetTimestamp();
const randomDigits8 = stamp.resetTimestamp();
const randomDigits9 = stamp.resetTimestamp();
```

Now, let's move all selectors to the `redminePage` object inside `redmine-page.js`. We will start from the login credentials:

```
let redminePage = {
    urlRedmine: 'http://demo.redmine.org/',
    emailRegularUser: `test_user_testcafe_poc${randomDigits1}@
sharklasers.com`,
    passwordRegularUser: 'test_user_testcafe_poc',
```

Now, let's add selectors for the page elements:

```
    linkLogin: '.login',
    inputUsername: '#username',
    inputPassword: '#password',
    buttonLogin: '[name="login"]',
    linkRegister: '.register',
    inputUserLogin: '#user_login',
    inputUserPassword: '#user_password',
    inputUserPasswordConfirmation: '#user_password_
confirmation',
    inputUserFirstName: '#user_firstname',
    inputUserLastName: '#user_lastname',
    inputUserMail: '#user_mail',
    buttonSubmit: '[value="Submit"]',
    blockNotification: '#flash_notice',
    blockLoggedAs: '#loggedas',
    linkLogout: '.logout',
    linkProjects: '#top-menu .projects',
    iconAdd: '.icon-add',
    inputProjectName: '#project_name',
    buttonCreate: '[value="Create"]',
    urlProjectSettings: `/projects/test_
project${randomDigits1}/settings`,
    link2TestProject: `[href*="/projects/test_
project${randomDigits2}"]`,

    // ...
```

And finally, let's enhance the `redminePage` object with properties containing the text:

```
    textFirstNameRegularUser: 'test_user',
    textLastNameRegularUser: 'testcafe_poc',
    textAccountActivated: 'Your account has been activated. You
```

```
can now log in.',
    text1ProjectName: `test_project${randomDigits1}`,
    text2ProjectName: `test_project${randomDigits2}`,

// ...

};

module.exports = redminePage;
```

As you can see, the URLs such as `http://demo.redmine.org/`, and the notification text strings such as `'Your account has been activated. You can now log in.'` can be easily refactored with `PageObjects` too.

Now, let's use `PageObject` elements in each of our tests. So, the updated `Redmine log in tests` fixture will look like this:

```
const { Selector, ClientFunction, Role } = require('testcafe');

const redminePage = require('./redmine-page.js');

const getPageUrl = ClientFunction(() => {
    return window.location.href;
});

const regularUser = Role(redminePage.urlRedmine, async (t) => {
    await t.click(redminePage.linkLogin)
        .typeText(redminePage.inputUsername, redminePage.
emailRegularUser)
        .typeText(redminePage.inputPassword, redminePage.
passwordRegularUser)
        .click(redminePage.buttonLogin);
});

fixture('Redmine log in tests').page(redminePage.urlRedmine);
```

The `Create a new user` test with `PageObject` elements will look like this:

```
test('Create a new user', async (t) => {
    await t.click(redminePage.linkRegister)
        .typeText(redminePage.inputUserLogin, redminePage.
emailRegularUser)
        .typeText(redminePage.inputUserPassword, redminePage.
passwordRegularUser)
        .typeText(redminePage.inputUserPasswordConfirmation,
redminePage.passwordRegularUser)
        .typeText(redminePage.inputUserFirstName, redminePage.
textFirstNameRegularUser)
        .typeText(redminePage.inputUserLastName, redminePage.
textLastNameRegularUser)
        .typeText(redminePage.inputUserMail, redminePage.
emailRegularUser)
        .click(redminePage.buttonSubmit)
        .expect(Selector(redminePage.blockNotification).
innerText).eql(redminePage.textAccountActivated);
});
```

The `Log in` and `Log out` tests will look like this:

```
test('Log in', async (t) => {
    await t.click(redminePage.linkLogin)
        .typeText(redminePage.inputUsername, redminePage.
emailRegularUser)
        .typeText(redminePage.inputPassword, redminePage.
passwordRegularUser)
        .click(redminePage.buttonLogin)
        .expect(Selector(redminePage.blockLoggedAs).exists).
ok();
});

test('Log out', async (t) => {
    await t.useRole(regularUser)
        .click(redminePage.linkLogout)
        .expect(Selector(redminePage.blockLoggedAs).exists).
notOk()
        .expect(Selector(redminePage.linkLogin).exists).ok();
});
```

Here is what the updated `Redmine entities creation tests` fixture will look like:

```
fixture('Redmine entities creation tests')
    .page(redminePage.urlRedmine)
    .beforeEach(async (t) => {
        await t.useRole(regularUser);
    });
```

The `Create a new project` and `Create a new issue` tests will look like this:

```
test('Create a new project', async (t) => {
    await t.click(redminePage.linkProjects)
        .click(redminePage.iconAdd)
        .typeText(redminePage.inputProjectName, redminePage.
text1ProjectName)
        .click(redminePage.buttonCreate)
        .expect(Selector(redminePage.blockNotification).
innerText).eql(redminePage.textSuccessfulCreation)
        .expect(getPageUrl()).contains(redminePage.
urlProjectSettings);
});

test('Create a new issue', async (t) => {
    await t.click(redminePage.linkProjects)
        .click(redminePage.iconAdd)
        .typeText(redminePage.inputProjectName, redminePage.
text2ProjectName)
        .click(redminePage.buttonCreate)
        .click(redminePage.linkProjects)
        .click(redminePage.link2TestProject)
        .click(redminePage.linkNewIssue)
        .typeText(redminePage.inputIssueSubject, redminePage.
text2IssueName)
        .typeText(redminePage.inputIssueDescription,
redminePage.text2IssueDescription)
        .click(redminePage.dropdownIssuePriority)
        .click(Selector(redminePage.optionIssuePriority).
withText(redminePage.textHigh))
        .click(redminePage.buttonCreate)
        .expect(Selector(redminePage.blockNotification).
innerText).contains(redminePage.textCreated);
});
```

> **Note**
>
> You can also review and download this file with all the tests updated to use PageObjects on GitHub: https://github.com/PacktPublishing/Modern-Web-Testing-with-TestCafe/blob/master/ch6/test-project/tests/basic-tests20.js.

In this section, we learned how to enhance tests with PageObjects and refactored our test project accordingly. Now, let's improve maintainability of the tests even further by adding functions to PageObject.

Improving PageObjects with functions

As we can observe in redmine-page.js, some of the properties inside PageObject still contain some repetitive code. Let's optimize our PageObject even more by moving such repetitive code into the separate functions:

```
// ...

const createButtonSelector = (text) => {
    return `[value="${text}"]`;
};
const createLinkTestProjectSelector = (randomDigits) => {
    return `[href*="/projects/test_project${randomDigits}"]`;
};
const createProjectNameText = (randomDigits) => {
    return `test_project${randomDigits}`;
};
const createIssueNameText = (randomDigits) => {
    return `Test issue ${randomDigits}`;
};
const createIssueDescriptionText = (randomDigits) => {
    return `Test issue description ${randomDigits}`;
};
const createIssueNameUpdatedText = (randomDigits) => {
    return `Issue ${randomDigits} updated`;
};

redminePage.buttonLogin = createButtonSelector('Login »');
redminePage.buttonSubmit = createButtonSelector('Submit');
redminePage.buttonCreate = createButtonSelector('Create');
redminePage.buttonAdd = createButtonSelector('Add');
```

Note that the `buttonLogin` selector was updated. Previously, it was `[name="login"]`, but now, the `createButtonSelector` function will return it as `[value="Login »"]`. This was done to generalize our selector's generation, so now the `buttonLogin` selector is created with the same `createButtonSelector` function as all the other button elements.

Let's now generate a group of selectors for the test project links:

```
redminePage.link2TestProject =
createLinkTestProjectSelector(randomDigits2);
redminePage.link3TestProject =
createLinkTestProjectSelector(randomDigits3);
redminePage.link4TestProject =
createLinkTestProjectSelector(randomDigits8);
redminePage.link5TestProject =
createLinkTestProjectSelector(randomDigits4);
redminePage.link6TestProject =
createLinkTestProjectSelector(randomDigits5);
redminePage.link7TestProject =
createLinkTestProjectSelector(randomDigits6);
redminePage.link8TestProject =
createLinkTestProjectSelector(randomDigits7);
redminePage.link9TestProject =
createLinkTestProjectSelector(randomDigits9);
```

Now, let's generate a group of texts for the test project name:

```
redminePage.text1ProjectName =
createProjectNameText(randomDigits1);
redminePage.text2ProjectName =
createProjectNameText(randomDigits2);
redminePage.text3ProjectName =
createProjectNameText(randomDigits3);
redminePage.text4ProjectName =
createProjectNameText(randomDigits8);
redminePage.text5ProjectName =
createProjectNameText(randomDigits4);
redminePage.text6ProjectName =
createProjectNameText(randomDigits5);
redminePage.text7ProjectName =
createProjectNameText(randomDigits6);
redminePage.text8ProjectName =
createProjectNameText(randomDigits7);
redminePage.text9ProjectName =
```

```
createProjectNameText(randomDigits9);
```

Finally, let's generate a group of object properties that will contain texts for the issue name (for example, `Test issue 1598717241841`) and issue description (for example, `Test issue description 1598717241841`):

```
redminePage.text2IssueName =
createIssueNameText(randomDigits2);
redminePage.text3IssueName =
createIssueNameText(randomDigits3);
redminePage.text5IssueName =
createIssueNameText(randomDigits4);
redminePage.text6IssueName =
createIssueNameText(randomDigits5);
redminePage.text7IssueName =
createIssueNameText(randomDigits6);
redminePage.text8IssueName =
createIssueNameText(randomDigits7);

redminePage.text2IssueDescription =
createIssueDescriptionText(randomDigits2);
redminePage.text3IssueDescription =
createIssueDescriptionText(randomDigits3);
redminePage.text5IssueDescription =
createIssueDescriptionText(randomDigits4);
redminePage.text6IssueDescription =
createIssueDescriptionText(randomDigits5);
redminePage.text7IssueDescription =
createIssueDescriptionText(randomDigits6);
redminePage.text8IssueDescription =
createIssueDescriptionText(randomDigits7);

redminePage.text5IssueNameUpdated =
createIssueNameUpdatedText(randomDigits4);
redminePage.text6IssueNameUpdated =
createIssueNameUpdatedText(randomDigits5);

module.exports = redminePage;
```

> **Note**
>
> You can also review and download this file with `PageObject` functions: `https://github.com/PacktPublishing/Modern-Web-Testing-with-TestCafe/blob/master/ch6/test-project/tests/redmine-page3.js`, and the corresponding file with tests: `https://github.com/PacktPublishing/Modern-Web-Testing-with-TestCafe/blob/master/ch6/test-project/tests/basic-tests21.js`.

So, now we have functions to create groups of similar selectors and texts. This technique is ultimately useful as a group of similar elements can be edited in one place by changing the corresponding function that creates them.

Summary

In this chapter, we explored how to use `Role` when logging in to speed up test execution, refactored the tests with `PageObject`, and improved `PageObject` with functions. Now we have a fast set of tests that are easy to maintain and expand upon (should that be necessary in the future). This knowledge can be utilized to refactor the existing tests, or to build a new robust and easy-to-maintain set of automated tests.

In the next chapter, we will wrap up the test project and have a quick peek into the future of TestCafe.

7

Findings from TestCafe

The main learning goal in this chapter is to optimize our test actions with functions and get familiar with how to use npm scripts to run the tests. We will also review the main direction of TestCafe framework development, along with some references to useful resources.

This knowledge will give us some additional ideas on how to refactor tests, how to run them more efficiently, and where to search for further improvements.

In this chapter, we're going to cover the following main topics:

- Taking a final step with test functions.
- Wrapping up the test project with npm scripts.
- Exploring TestCafe development and future plans.
- Additional references to useful resources.

Technical requirements

All code examples for this chapter can be found on GitHub: `https://github.com/PacktPublishing/Modern-Web-Testing-with-TestCafe/blob/master/ch7`.

Taking a final step with test functions

The tests that we created consist of chains of actions. Some of them, such as the Creating a new project test, are still being repeated. So, one final logical step to take will be to separate such sequences of actions into the functions. Let's see how this can be achieved with the createNewProject, createNewIssue, and uploadFile functions inside redmine-page.js:

```
const { Selector, ClientFunction, Role, t } =
require('testcafe');
const { stamp } = require('js-automation-tools');

// ...

redminePage.getPageUrl = ClientFunction(() => {
    return window.location.href;
});
redminePage.regularUser = Role(redminePage.urlRedmine, async
(t) => {
    await t.click(redminePage.linkLogin)
        .typeText(redminePage.inputUsername, redminePage.
emailRegularUser)
        .typeText(redminePage.inputPassword, redminePage.
passwordRegularUser)
        .click(redminePage.buttonLogin);
});
```

As you can see, we moved getPageUrl and regularUser to redmine-page.js as it is quite convenient to have all the utility functions concentrated in one file.

Now, let's add the createNewProject function, which will contain all the actions to create a new project:

```
redminePage.createNewProject = async (textProjectName) => {
    await t.click(redminePage.linkProjects)
        .click(redminePage.iconAdd)
        .typeText(redminePage.inputProjectName,
textProjectName)
        .click(redminePage.buttonCreate);
};
```

There is one more function to add, which will contain all the actions to create a new issue:

```
redminePage.createNewIssue = async (
    linkTestProject, textIssueName, textIssueDescription
    ) => {
    await t.click(redminePage.linkProjects)
        .click(linkTestProject)
        .click(redminePage.linkNewIssue)
        .typeText(redminePage.inputIssueSubject, textIssueName)
        .typeText(redminePage.inputIssueDescription,
textIssueDescription)
        .click(redminePage.dropdownIssuePriority)
        .click(Selector(redminePage.optionIssuePriority).
withText(redminePage.textHigh))
        .click(redminePage.buttonCreate);
};
```

And finally, add the function that contains all the actions to upload a file:

```
redminePage.uploadFile = async (linkTestProject) => {
    await t.click(redminePage.linkProjects)
        .click(linkTestProject)
        .click(redminePage.linkFiles)
        .click(redminePage.iconAdd)
        .setFilesToUpload(redminePage.inputChooseFiles,
redminePage.pathToFile)
        .click(redminePage.buttonAdd);
};

module.exports = redminePage;
```

> **Note**
>
> You can also review and download this file on GitHub: https://
> github.com/PacktPublishing/Modern-Web-Testing-
> with-TestCafe/blob/master/ch7/test-project/tests/
> redmine-page4.js.

Now, the updated `Create a new project` test will look like this:

```
const { Selector } = require('testcafe');

const redminePage = require('./redmine-page.js');

// ...

fixture('Redmine entities creation tests')
    .page(redminePage.urlRedmine)
    .beforeEach(async (t) => {
        await t.useRole(redminePage.regularUser);
    });

test('Create a new project', async (t) => {
    await redminePage.createNewProject(redminePage.
text1ProjectName);
    await t.expect(Selector(redminePage.blockNotification).
innerText).eql(redminePage.textSuccessfulCreation)
        .expect(redminePage.getPageUrl()).contains(redminePage.
urlProjectSettings);
});
```

As you probably noticed, now, only `Selector` is required from `testcafe`, as `ClientFunction`, `Role`, and `t` were moved to `redmine-page.js`. In addition, we are now using `redminePage.regularUser` instead of just `regularUser` - this is due to moving the `regularUser` function to `redmine-page.js`.

The updated `Create a new issue` test will look like this:

```
test('Create a new issue', async (t) => {
    await redminePage.createNewProject(redminePage.
text2ProjectName);
    await redminePage.createNewIssue(
        redminePage.link2TestProject,
        redminePage.text2IssueName,
        redminePage.text2IssueDescription
    );
    await t.expect(Selector(redminePage.blockNotification).
innerText).contains(redminePage.textCreated);
});
```

The `Verify that the issue is displayed on a project page` test will also look shorter now, as we are using the `createNewProject` and `createNewIssue` functions inside it to create corresponding entities:

```
test('Verify that the issue is displayed on a project page',
async (t) => {
    await redminePage.createNewProject(redminePage.
text3ProjectName);
    await redminePage.createNewIssue(
        redminePage.link3TestProject,
        redminePage.text3IssueName,
        redminePage.text3IssueDescription
    );
    await t.click(redminePage.linkProjects)
        .click(redminePage.link3TestProject)
        .click(redminePage.linkIssues)
        .expect(Selector(redminePage.linkIssueName).innerText).
contains(redminePage.text3IssueName);
});
```

In the `Upload a file` test, we will utilize the `createNewProject` and `uploadFile` functions so that it will look more compact, too:

```
test('Upload a file', async (t) => {
    await redminePage.createNewProject(redminePage.
text4ProjectName);
    await redminePage.uploadFile(redminePage.link4TestProject);
    await t.expect(Selector(redminePage.linkFileName).
innerText).eql(redminePage.textFileName)
        .expect(Selector(redminePage.blockDigest).innerText).
eql(redminePage.textChecksum);
});
```

Here is how the updated `Edit the issue` test with the `createNewProject` and `createNewIssue` functions will appear:

```
// ...

test('Edit the issue', async (t) => {
    await redminePage.createNewProject(redminePage.
text5ProjectName);
    await redminePage.createNewIssue(
        redminePage.link5TestProject,
        redminePage.text5IssueName,
```

```
            redminePage.text5IssueDescription
    );
    await t.click(redminePage.linkProjects)
        .click(redminePage.link5TestProject)
        .click(redminePage.linkIssues)
        .click(Selector(redminePage.linkIssueName).
withText(redminePage.text5IssueName))
        .click(redminePage.iconEdit)
        .selectText(redminePage.inputIssueSubject)
        .pressKey(redminePage.keyDelete)
        .typeText(redminePage.inputIssueSubject, redminePage.
text5IssueNameUpdated)
        .click(redminePage.dropdownIssuePriority)
        .click(Selector(redminePage.optionIssuePriority).
withText(redminePage.textNormal))
        .click(redminePage.buttonSubmit)
        .expect(Selector(redminePage.blockNotification).
innerText).eql(redminePage.textSuccessfulUpdate);
});
```

And the refactored `Verify that the updated issue is displayed on a project` page test with the `createNewProject` and `createNewIssue` functions will now look like this:

```
test('Verify that the updated issue is displayed on a project
page', async (t) => {
    await redminePage.createNewProject(redminePage.
text6ProjectName);
    await redminePage.createNewIssue(
        redminePage.link6TestProject,
        redminePage.text6IssueName,
        redminePage.text6IssueDescription
    );
    await t.click(redminePage.linkProjects)
        .click(redminePage.link6TestProject)
        .click(redminePage.linkIssues)
        .click(Selector(redminePage.linkIssueName).
withText(redminePage.text6IssueName))
        .click(redminePage.iconEdit)
        .selectText(redminePage.inputIssueSubject)
        .pressKey(redminePage.keyDelete)
        .typeText(redminePage.inputIssueSubject, redminePage.
text6IssueNameUpdated)
```

```
        .click(redminePage.dropdownIssuePriority)
        .click(Selector(redminePage.optionIssuePriority).
withText(redminePage.textNormal))
        .click(redminePage.buttonSubmit)
        .click(redminePage.linkIssues)
        .expect(Selector(redminePage.linkIssueName).innerText).
eql(redminePage.text6IssueNameUpdated);
});
```

The `Search for the issue` test will also benefit from utilizing the
`createNewProject` and `createNewIssue` functions as it will become significantly
shorter:

```
test('Search for the issue', async (t) => {
    await redminePage.createNewProject(redminePage.
text7ProjectName);
    await redminePage.createNewIssue(
        redminePage.link7TestProject,
        redminePage.text7IssueName,
        redminePage.text7IssueDescription
    );
    await t.navigateTo(redminePage.urlRedmineSearch)
        .typeText(redminePage.inputSearch, redminePage.
text7IssueName)
        .click(redminePage.buttonSubmit)
        .expect(Selector(redminePage.blockSearchResults).
innerText).contains(redminePage.text7IssueName);
});
```

And finally, here is what the refactored `Delete the issue` and `Delete the file`
tests will look like:

```
// ...

test('Delete the issue', async (t) => {
    await redminePage.createNewProject(redminePage.
text8ProjectName);
    await redminePage.createNewIssue(
        redminePage.link8TestProject,
        redminePage.text8IssueName,
        redminePage.text8IssueDescription
    );
    await t.click(redminePage.linkProjects)
        .click(redminePage.link8TestProject)
```

```
        .click(redminePage.linkIssues)
        .click(Selector(redminePage.linkIssueName).
withText(redminePage.text8IssueName))
        .setNativeDialogHandler(() => true)
        .click(redminePage.iconDelete)
        .expect(Selector(redminePage.linkIssueName).
withText(redminePage.text8IssueName).exists).notOk()
        .expect(Selector(redminePage.blockNoData).innerText).
eql(redminePage.textNoData);
});

test('Delete the file', async (t) => {
    await redminePage.createNewProject(redminePage.
text9ProjectName);
    await redminePage.uploadFile(redminePage.link9TestProject);
    await t.click(redminePage.linkProjects)
        .click(redminePage.link9TestProject)
        .click(redminePage.linkFiles)
        .setNativeDialogHandler(() => true)
        .click(Selector(redminePage.linkFileName).
withText(redminePage.textFileName).parent(redminePage.
blockFile).find(redminePage.buttonAction).withAttribute('data-
method', redminePage.dataMethodDelete))
        .expect(Selector(redminePage.linkFileName).
withText(redminePage.textFileName).exists).notOk()
        .expect(Selector(redminePage.blockDigest).
withText(redminePage.textChecksum).exists).notOk();
});
```

> **Note**
>
> You can also review and download this file on GitHub: `https://github.com/PacktPublishing/Modern-Web-Testing-with-TestCafe/blob/master/ch7/test-project/tests/basic-tests22.js`.

So, we have optimized our set of tests to be granular and utilize functions instead of repeated actions. Now, let's wrap up the test project with npm scripts.

Wrapping up the test project with npm scripts

As we have finished refactoring our tests, let's see how to run them more efficiently. As we recall from *Chapter 3, Setting Up the Environment*, where we initiated `package.json`, and *Chapter 4, Building a Test Suite with TestCafe*, where we added the `js-automation-tools` library, our basic `package.json` file currently looks like this:

```
{
  "name": "test-project",
  "version": "1.0.0",
  "description": "",
  "main": "index.js",
  "scripts": {
    "test": "echo \"Error: no test specified\" && exit 1"
  },
  "keywords": [],
  "author": "",
  "license": "ISC",
  "devDependencies": {
    "js-automation-tools": "^1.0.5",
    "testcafe": "^1.8.7"
  }
}
```

We are currently running our tests by executing the following command:

```
$ npx testcafe chrome tests/basic-tests.js
```

Or, as we discussed in *Chapter 5, Improving the Tests*, we utilize a double dash debug-on-fail flag to make our life easier while developing new tests (this will pause the test when it fails and will allow you to view the tested page and determine the cause of the fail):

```
$ npx testcafe chrome tests/basic-tests.js --debug-on-fail
```

We can also use one additional flag:`--speed` (sets the rate of test execution) – to reduce the test execution speed for debugging:

```
$ npx testcafe chrome tests/basic-tests.js --debug-on-fail
--speed 0.8
```

It is starting to look quite long now, isn't it? To overcome this problem, we can use npm scripts. Let's create a `test-debug` alias inside `package.json` to launch tests with debugging flags:

```json
{
  "name": "test-project",
  "version": "1.0.0",
  "description": "",
  "main": "index.js",
  "scripts": {
    "test-debug": "testcafe chrome tests/basic-tests.js
--debug-on-fail --speed 0.8"
  },
  "keywords": [],
  "author": "",
  "license": "ISC",
  "devDependencies": {
    "js-automation-tools": "^1.0.5",
    "testcafe": "^1.8.7"
  }
}
```

So, now we can run our tests with **debugging flags** by executing a short command with the alias that we just created:

```
$ npm run test-debug
```

As we have discussed how to use npm scripts to add commands for local test debugging, let's now imagine that we will also need to run our tests on a **continuous integration system (CI system)**. It would be good to rerun any failed test three times, just to be on the safe side and eliminate any possible flakiness. So, let's add a `--quarantine-mode` flag:

```json
{
  "name": "test-project",
  "version": "1.0.0",
  "description": "",
  "main": "index.js",
  "scripts": {
    "test-ci": "testcafe chrome tests/basic-tests.js
--quarantine-mode",
    "test-debug": "testcafe chrome tests/basic-tests.js
--debug-on-fail --speed 0.8"
  },
  "keywords": [],
```

```
  "author": "",
  "license": "ISC",
  "devDependencies": {
    "js-automation-tools": "^1.0.5",
    "testcafe": "^1.8.7"
  }
}
```

> **Note**
>
> You can also review and download this file on GitHub: `https://github.com/PacktPublishing/Modern-Web-Testing-with-TestCafe/blob/master/ch7/test-project/package.json`.

So, now we can run our tests on CI by executing a short and simple command:

```
$ npm run test-ci
```

To sum up, in this section, we discussed how to create short aliases for the local and remote (continuous integration) commands with npm scripts.

Now, let's explore how to keep a finger on the pulse of TestCafe development and where to look for further improvements.

Exploring TestCafe development and future plans

The birth of TestCafe can be traced back to early 2010, when developers from DevExpress started working on it. Initially, when released in 2013, it was a commercial testing framework. In 2016, it was decided to open source the core of TestCafe. Since then, there have been more than 760,000 downloads per month and the figures are still growing. DevExpress also released a commercial testing IDE called TestCafe Studio (`https://www.devexpress.com/products/testcafestudio/`), which was built on top of the open source TestCafe core. So, it looks like TestCafe is here to stay. DevExpress will keep developing it because this will add new features to TestCafe Studio.

Let's recap some of the advantages of TestCafe:

- Open source.
- Easy and fast installation.
- Headless testing.

- Cross-platform and cross-browser out of the box.

- Supports one of the most popular programming languages for web development: JavaScript/TypeScript.

- A clear, flexible, and well-documented API.

- Smart assertion and automatic waiting mechanisms out of the box.

- Free custom plugins for browser providers, framework-specific selectors, custom reporters, Cucumber support, and so on.

As for the future direction of development for TestCafe, according to the roadmap (`https://devexpress.github.io/testcafe/roadmap/`), there is a plan to support API testing by adding methods for sending HTTP requests and checking the response details. In addition to this, the TestCafe team is actively working on multiple browser windows feature and a plan is afoot to improve the TestCafe debugging flow further.

One more piece of advice that is definitely worth mentioning: keep an eye on TestCafe changelog (`https://github.com/DevExpress/testcafe/blob/master/CHANGELOG.md`). It contains tons of useful information about new features and updates. This way, you will always know when a new version gets released, and what to expect from it.

As we have reviewed the development of TestCafe and touched on its future plans, let's now explore some resources that can be of use in terms of further test automation with TestCafe.

Additional references to useful resources

Here are some great sources of information on TestCafe:

- **TestCafe documentation**: `https://devexpress.github.io/testcafe/documentation/reference/`.

- **TestCafe changelog**: `https://github.com/DevExpress/testcafe/blob/master/CHANGELOG.md`.

- **TestCafe future roadmap**: `https://devexpress.github.io/testcafe/roadmap/` and `https://github.com/DevExpress/testcafe/projects`.

- **TestCafe Team Blog**: `https://devexpress.github.io/testcafe/media/team-blog/`.

- **Stack Overflow filter for the most recent questions regarding TestCafe**: `https://stackoverflow.com/questions/tagged/testcafe`.

Summary

In this chapter, we explored how to optimize test actions with functions, and how to use npm scripts to run the tests. We also reviewed the development of the TestCafe framework, and some references to useful resources. These skills and lessons are intended to help you with any further test automation development by highlighting a number of ideas on how to refactor tests, how to run them more effectively, and where to look for further improvements.

This wraps up our fruitful exploration of TestCafe, the rising star of test automation. I hope that you enjoyed it and will continue using this magnificent tool in your future projects!

`Packt.com`

Subscribe to our online digital library for full access to over 7,000 books and videos, as well as industry leading tools to help you plan your personal development and advance your career. For more information, please visit our website.

Why subscribe?

- Spend less time learning and more time coding with practical eBooks and Videos from over 4,000 industry professionals

- Improve your learning with Skill Plans built especially for you

- Get a free eBook or video every month

- Fully searchable for easy access to vital information

- Copy and paste, print, and bookmark content

Did you know that Packt offers eBook versions of every book published, with PDF and ePub files available? You can upgrade to the eBook version at `packt.com` and as a print book customer, you are entitled to a discount on the eBook copy. Get in touch with us at `customercare@packtpub.com` for more details.

At `www.packt.com`, you can also read a collection of free technical articles, sign up for a range of free newsletters, and receive exclusive discounts and offers on Packt books and eBooks.

Other Books You May Enjoy

If you enjoyed this book, you may be interested in these other books by Packt:

Node Web Development, Fifth Edition
David Herron
ISBN: 978-1-83898-757-2

- Install and use Node.js 14 and Express 4.17 for both web development and deployment

- Implement RESTful web services using the Restify framework

- Develop, test, and deploy microservices using Docker, Docker Swarm, and Node.js, on AWS EC2 using Terraform

- Get up to speed with using data storage engines such as MySQL, SQLite3, and MongoDB

- Test your web applications using unit testing with Mocha, and headless browser testing with Puppeteer

- Implement HTTPS using Let's Encrypt and enhance application security with Helmet

Svelte 3 Up and Running

Alessandro Segala

ISBN: 978-1-83921-362-5

- Understand why Svelte 3 is the go-to framework for building static web apps that offer great UX
- Explore the tool setup that makes it easier to build and debug Svelte apps
- Scaffold your web project and build apps using the Svelte framework
- Create Svelte components using the Svelte template syntax and its APIs
- Combine Svelte components to build apps that solve complex real-world problems
- Use Svelte's built-in animations and transitions for creating components
- Implement routing for client-side single-page applications (SPAs)
- Perform automated testing and deploy your Svelte apps, using CI/CD when applicable

Packt is searching for authors like you

If you're interested in becoming an author for Packt, please visit authors. packtpub.com and apply today. We have worked with thousands of developers and tech professionals, just like you, to help them share their insight with the global tech community. You can make a general application, apply for a specific hot topic that we are recruiting an author for, or submit your own idea.

Leave a review - let other readers know what you think

Please share your thoughts on this book with others by leaving a review on the site that you bought it from. If you purchased the book from Amazon, please leave us an honest review on this book's Amazon page. This is vital so that other potential readers can see and use your unbiased opinion to make purchasing decisions, we can understand what our customers think about our products, and our authors can see your feedback on the title that they have worked with Packt to create. It will only take a few minutes of your time, but is valuable to other potential customers, our authors, and Packt. Thank you!

Index

www.ingramcontent.com/pod-product-compliance
Lightning Source LLC
Chambersburg PA
CBHW060140060326
40690CB00018B/3928